BUSINESS WRITING THAT COUNTS!™

Dr. Julie Miller

BOOK PUBLISHERS NETWORK

Book Publishers Network
P.O. Box 2256
Bothell, WA, 98041
PH 425-483-3040

First printing, 1999
Second printing, 2000, revised
Third printing, 2002
Fourth printing, 2003, completely revised
Fifth printing, 2006, completely revised

Library of Congress Cataloging-in-Publication Data
Miller, Julie Pascal

Business writing that counts!/ Julie Miller ; Jonathan Todd,
contributing author. -- 4th ed. -- Bothell, WA : Book Publishers Network,
2004.

p. cm

Includes bibliography references and index.
ISBN: 1-887542-37-X
1. Business writing.   2. Business comunication. I. Todd,
Jonathan. II. Title.

HF5718.3 .M55 2004   2003112991
808/.6665--DC22   0401

Grateful acknowledgement is made for permission granted by Pantheon
Books for excerpts from *Bird by Bird* by Anne Lamont, 1994; and by *The
Seattle Times*, 1996-2000; permission has also been requested from *Travel
and Leisure* magazine.

Manufactured in the United States
10 9 8 7 6

Editor: Karyn Frazier
Cover: Eran Becker
Interior: Stephanie Martindale
Index: Carolyn Acheson

DEDICATIONS

Dr. Julie Miller

To my extraordinary and ever-patient husband—his love and support sustain me. To my dear and generous father, whose mentoring challenged and empowered me. To my precious and beloved mother—she would have been so proud.

Jonathan Todd

To my wife, Ilona—your calm power, focused direction and deep undercurrent of love has always been the wind beneath my wings. To my daughter, Natasha—you are simply the brightest light in the universe. I can't wait for the rest of the world to discover you! Finally, the deepest respect and admiration for my parents—you have always done the right thing, have always been there for me, and have always known the secret of silent parental communication during those most important moments in life. I am a most fortunate man.

ACKNOWLEDGEMENTS

Dr. Julie Miller

To Karyn Frazier for her thoughtful edits to this fourth edition.

To all my clients, whose writing frustrations and successes continue to add to the depth and breadth of this book.

Jonathan Todd

To Julie Miller, who has written one of the most important books on writing ever to grace the business bookshelf. When I first read her work, I was profoundly struck by how useful and elegant her system is. It is an honor to be asked to contribute to this edition. A special thanks to our publisher, Sheryn Hara, for her publishing prowess and great people skills. To those who influence my personal and professional life so much—Ben, Girshon, Michael, Mick, Steven, and the SabreMark, Inc., team, my deepest thanks.

CONTENTS

CHAPTER 1
GET ORGANIZED
1

CHAPTER 2
GET STARTED
27

CHAPTER 3
GET IT DONE
55

CHAPTER 4
GET SMART
89

CHAPTER 5
GET IT WRITE
127

CHAPTER 6
GET WRITING
147

Special Section by Jonathan Todd
BUSINESS WRITING THAT SELLS!
193

APPENDIX
241

INDEX
257

ABOUT THE AUTHORS & SPECIAL RESOURCES
271

Introduction to

Business Writing That Counts!

This millennium has been coined the "writing-est" of times... Words fly over the airwaves at the blink of an eye. With each new technological advance, the speed of business increases and so does the pressure from customers who demand instantaneous responses. Getting your messages and documents written and sent *quickly* is one issue; making them interesting, clear, concise, and powerful is another. *Business Writing That Counts!* helps you do both.

Let's be honest. Writing does not top the "favorites" list of many people. Bright, hard-working individuals invent the most amazing excuses for not getting to it because they view writing as difficult and frustrating work. *Business Writing That Counts!* makes the writing process easier and less painful by teaching you a simple system to get it done quickly!

Business Writing That Counts! also provides practical strategies for your work world. The consequences of ineffective communication are legendary. Poorly written documents create unnecessary waste—of time, money, energy. And the amount of lost revenue due to missed opportunities is inestimable. Whether you write newsletters, memos, e-mails, proposals, or reports for large companies, medium-sized companies, or home-based businesses, this book will help you *get organized, get started, and get writing.*

My goal? As corny as it sounds, I want you to feel empowered, to know that if you can talk, you can write!

I have attempted to make my book user-friendly and pragmatic. Read it sequentially, learning and building skills as you go, or pick it up and read any chapter of interest or concern.

The first three chapters set the foundation with a quick and easy brainstorming process, a unique numbering system, and the permission to break writing rules we were sworn to uphold. The last three help you refine your writing, address common business writing concerns, and present you with invaluable writing tips.

Business Writing That Counts! has seven main benefits for you, the reader. It will:

- Save you time, which ultimately saves you money
- Increase your productivity
- Make your writing more interesting
- Provide you with an elegant numbering system that you can apply no matter what you have to write.
- Show you how to simplify your writing
- Focus your message on your reader
- Enhance your company's reputation as well as your own

Turn the page and let's get started. And welcome to the world of quick, easy, and powerful writing.

Here's to good writing!

Author's note

This fourth edition of *Business Writing That Counts!* contains a special comprehensive section on sales writing presented by one of the top marketing and sales experts in the country, Jonathan Todd. In *Business Writing That Sells!*, you will to learn from the best how to write what sells. This bonus section offers you an exclusive opportunity to enhance your sales writing and get the results you want. Don't miss it!

CHAPTER ONE

GET ORGANIZED

Quit Circling the Computer!

It's all about the bottom line these days. In this current business environment, maximizing efficiency and reducing costs have become critical. When you write, you must get to the heart of the issue—quickly and concisely. Whether you write e-mails all day or craft expert reports, reducing your writing time and increasing your productivity is essential—and expected.

Few people enjoy sitting down to put on paper what could be *said* in less than half the time. And for most of us, talking with peers or clients takes less effort and causes fewer panic attacks than writing does. But with the Internet fast becoming the primary venue for communication, doing business in writing is a given, not an option. E-mails, memos, performance reviews, letters, business plans, proposals, status reports, white papers, executive summaries, Web pages...the list goes on and on.

> Writing is easy. All you have to do is sit down . . . and wait for drops of blood to form on your forehead.
> —Gene Fowler

What if I told you that you could approach writing tasks with the same ease and speed you do conversation? Well, you can. Read on.

Instantaneous is just too darn slow

Businesses pressure employees to deliver and deliver fast. Writing on demand is a constant requirement and ineffective writers have no place to hide if their writing skills remain sub par!

While technology gives us the ability to soar like an eagle, it also saddles us with the burden of the albatross. Thanks to the instancy of the Internet, we can respond with lightning speed; unfortunately, these quick communiqués often come at the expense of clarity of thought. This constant demand for immediacy raises the stakes *and* our blood pressure.

When you don't have enough time to spend on what you write, you leave yourself open to all sorts of calamities. Have you ever found yourself stuck with any of the following unwanted results?

- Missed opportunities because the writing team lacked efficient and effective skills
- Higher labor costs from rewriting unclear documents
- Damaged reputations because of poorly written documents
- Thinner bottom lines when proposals are rejected due to poor quality

Caution: Not spending time to make your writing clear, cogent, and concise may be hazardous to your career or business health!

Writing eats up time

We also know *the time* that writing can take, gobbling it up like Pavarotti at a bake sale. The entire process generates huge amounts of fear, worry, or procrastination, usually involves criticism (by ourselves and others), and takes *a great deal of time* to organize. A recent client of mine, the owner of a placement service, told of his frustration in getting out a letter to his customers regarding a new billing procedure. He said, "Something's wrong with this picture. I just spent three hours writing three paragraphs people will read in three minutes! Not to mention the cost of mailing the darn things!"

Why did it take him so long to write a brief letter? Because he invested too much time on the *start-up*—meaning those initial organizing steps. He had no efficient writing system in place that would help him quickly arrange his thoughts and get the document out to his customers.

So we circle the computer or clean every nook and cranny in the office.

For most of us, just getting started is the most difficult part of the writing process. So we circle the computer, schmooze with coworkers, get another latté, clean every nook and cranny in the office—*anything* to avoid getting started.

Why? Two reasons:
- We don't know where to begin; *and . . .*
- We get hung up on following (let alone *remembering*) the sacred rules of the writing process.

What stops you in your tracks?

Review the excuses below for not getting started. Do any of these ring true for you?

❑ I'm so lousy at writing.
❑ It takes too much time.

- ❑ I never know what to say.
- ❑ I'm not *into* suffering.
- ❑ I'm scared what my writing will reveal about me.
- ❑ I become so overwhelmed with the task I can't get organized.
- ❑ I'd rather *call* than write to my client.
- ❑ It's not my area of strength.
- ❑ I need lots of creative time.

So enough already! You've admitted your frustrations and fears. Now, just shrug them off and jump right in. You're going to have fun along the way—I promise.

In this first chapter, you will learn how to overcome the blank-screen syndrome and quickly organize your thoughts by using **Idea Maps**. You will also gain an additional benefit: *permission* to break some of the rules drilled into you in school.

For that reason, I'll start by giving you immediate dispensation to **get going and quit circling the computer!**

Rule-Breaker Number One: Throw Out the Formal Outline!

We've all had a teacher sometime during our school career who believed in strict adherence to the rules. Mine? Sister Mary John, Her mission in life? To cram into our pointy little heads *the writing rules*—rules for diagramming, punctuation, dependent and independent clauses, prepositional phrases, nouns, verbs, *ad nauseam.* Following the rules, focusing on the mechanics, and writing correctly reigned supreme but didn't always make our writing very interesting.

Admittedly, learning those important fundamentals gave us the basics; however, *fun* was not part of the drill-and-skill regimen. Those rules seemed designed to expose and catalog the weaknesses in our writing instead of acting as powerful and positive tools to help us along the way. The lingering effect today remains that these rules can keep us from getting organized, getting started, and getting writing.

Sister Mary John had one cardinal rule in particular that could never be violated: We could not scribble one word onto paper until we had produced approved outlines. (*So we wrote the paper first and then did the outline.*)

Who remembers the rules to formal outlining, anyway? And who cares?! Often outlining seems like a painful, laborious, frustrating, and completely unnecessary exercise.

Even more important, outlining sets up a prescribed approach to your topic before you have determined your direction. But worst of all, while you're trying to remember whether to use Roman numerals or lower case letters, parentheses or periods, you find yourself stalling, putting off the real task of writing.

The real issue, then, is knowing which rules you can break.

As you go through this book, you will learn how to write with competence, confidence, *and* speed. And, best of all, you can thumb your nose at some of those rules!

Idea Mapping:
A Simple Path to Creativity

The easiest way to reduce your start-up time and *gain productivity time* comes through moving beyond the formal outline process to an **Idea Map!** What's an Idea Map? It's an illustration of your ideas on any topic, a graphic display of your thinking that mirrors how your brain works—in a non-linear, multidimensional way. Various names for creating this visual tool include "mind mapping," "clustering" or "webbing." I call it **Idea Mapping.**

You can apply Idea Mapping to any kind of writing project to give structure to your ideas while unlocking your creative genius.

Perhaps you know your topic and just want a faster system for getting your ideas down. Maybe you're the financial analyst organizing data on trends in the timber industry, *or* you need to generate new ideas for a software company developing an employee compensation package. Idea Mapping works.

Why? Because paying attention to the rules can literally stop you before you get started.

Why? Because formal outlining takes too much time and diverts your focus!

Why? Because your best ideas—your most creative ideas—come when you let go in an unedited, disorderly, free-flowing stream of consciousness.

Why? Because you want those good, creative ideas in your document.

Our thinking processes have always yielded riches when we've approached things openly, letting free associations form into new ideas. Many would argue that we've used such a small part of our mental capacity because of our insistence on linear thinking.

-Margaret Wheatley

Chart your own map

When you have to prepare reports, proposals, RFPs, business cases, even speeches, Idea Mapping provides a shortcut to simpler, more efficient organization.

Put your ideas down without judgment or evaluation.

Like brainstorming, Idea Mapping keeps you focused and allows you to ignore the internal *naysayers* as you freely generate your ideas. By staying *focused* you eliminate a big time-waster—going back again and again to reorganize your thoughts.

Before we go through the nine steps, let's look at a completed Idea Map. A speech coach drafted this example to capture his observations about a sales presentation. Can you see how this quickly the ideas took shape *before* any structured writing process began?

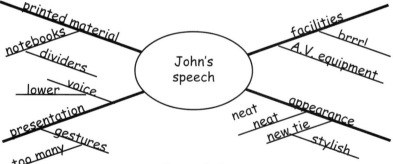

Example A
A critique sheet of a speech used during John's debriefing.

Dr. Julie Tip:
Idea Mapping can generate twice as many ideas as the conventional listing and outlining of topics. Why? Because according to the latest research, our brain does not necessarily process information in lists. Create Idea Maps and free your brain.

In the following pages, you will learn nine easy steps for organizing your ideas without becoming bogged down by the rule-laden formal outline process. No magic—just practical, visual guides. Once you practice these steps, in no time you'll Idea Map a letter in *five minutes* flat! Or quickly create marketing material that drives customers to your door. Stay tuned for those details in the *Business Writing That Sells!* section.

The Steps

1 **Start with a blank piece of paper and a pencil or pen.** Consider using a legal-size pad, a white board, a flip chart. Your brainstormed ideas will be graphically displayed on the Idea Map.

2 **Put down the main idea you want to write about in the center of your paper.** Use a single word or a phrase (abbreviations are fine) and draw a circle around it. (Figure 1) Since I've stressed the importance of saving time, the main idea of my Idea Map is *time management habits.*

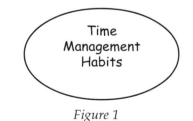

Time
Management
Habits

Figure 1

Dr. Julie Tip:
For meetings or group sessions: Use an easel-size pad of paper or a white board for large group projects. Everyone can see it. Use sticky notes to easily move your ideas under different branches.

3 Next, consider these reader-focused questions:

❑ *What is your purpose, your objective, the goal of your document?* To persuade, explain, sell, apologize, inform, or entertain? Decide what results you want from your message.

❑ *Who is your reader?* What does he/she *need to* know (rather than, what do *I* want to tell him/her)? Keep an image of your reader in your mind's eye. How does he/she feel or think about your topic?

❑ *What do you want the reader to do with the information?* Sue? Send money? Throw your communication into the circular file? Call you?

I can't write without a reader. It's precisely like a kiss—you can't do it alone.

- John Cheever

The reader remains at the heart of your writing. Unless you write to the reader, don't even pick up the pen, don't even put your fingers to the keyboard! The whole *purpose* of your document must be to engage the *reader* so that he/she *does* something with your information.

4 Now, start filling in the Idea Map by answering this mapping question: *What major points, key concepts, or important ideas can I address about my topic?* A mapping question helps you focus your topic and starts you down the right path as you map. (See mapping question for time management example on the page 10.)

5 As you brainstorm your major points, draw lines out from the circled main idea. (Figure 2) Write down words and phrases rapidly on those lines (*no sentences—*they slow you down). Keep those freewheeling ideas coming. They can

hitchhike on each other. One idea will trigger another and then another.

Don't make judgments as to whether the points completely fit with the topic. You will decide later which ideas you will keep.

To you, this process may seem random or chaotic or disorderly or messy or informal. It is all of these! Keep that left side of your brain quiet. Relax and just jot the ideas down anyway.

On the lines radiating out from your circled main idea, you will fill in the *major* points, the key concepts about your main idea. Write down words and phrases that answer the mapping question in step #4 (above).

In this example, I've mapped the important habits that help manage one's time.

Mapping Question: *What would be important time management habits to practice?*

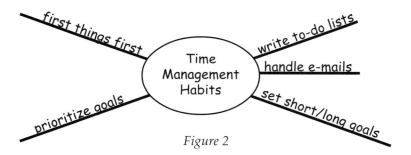

Figure 2

6 As you generate ideas that further support or detail your major points, start adding lines (twigs to your branches) with words or phrases. These become your details and examples that add increasingly specific information to your major points. (Figure 3)

*❘ Note: Your ideas will not necessarily come to you sequentially.
❘ You'll think of a major point or minor detail about one idea
that will trigger an idea about something else. Perhaps some of
your ideas may not seem to fit under any of the branches. Write
them down anyway on the Idea Map. Let your creativity flow!*

What data, examples, explanations, clarifications, or
descriptions about your major points can you use to support
the main idea? In this example, I list points (twigs) that clarify
ways you can acquire these time management habits.

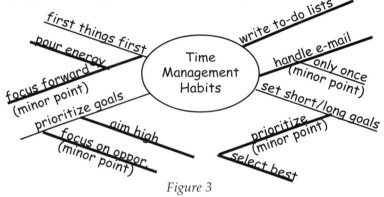

Figure 3

Remember: Try not to edit yourself; instead, continue
to generate major points and minor details until you have
finished. That may sound like a silly statement, but you'll
know when you're done. (Allot at least five to ten minutes
for this exercise.) Either you'll run out of ideas or you will
be very clear about what you want to write.

7 **Decide what major points will stay and which
ones will go.** When you're finished, step back
from the Idea Map. Become a critical thinker.
Determine what minor points to combine or
delete or which actually belong under
another point.

8 **Circle the individual big branches with the
major and minor points on them.** This will make

Blocked? Can't think of anything? Just draw some blank lines radiating out from your main idea. With this simple act, you release the mental logjam in your brain. Why? Because your brain cannot stand incompleteness and it will eventually think of a word to put on that line. Amazing, huh?

it easy for you to see the number of points you plan to make in your report, letter, speech, or proposal. (Figure 4)

9   **Last, try to determine the best order in which you will write your document.** Prioritize your ideas by placing a number next to each circled branch. (Figure 4) Later on in this chapter, I'll show you additional ways to organize information.

A completed (and circled) Idea Map

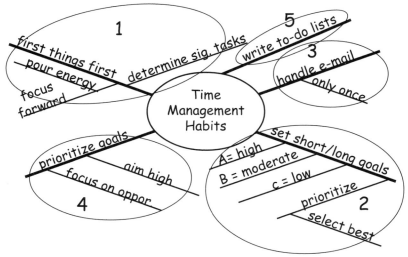

Figure 4

In this Idea Map, you will find:

- The topic for the magazine article
- Key concepts (habits) about time management
- Abbreviated words and phrases
- Major points with supporting details and examples
- Numbers indicating the best order for the points to appear in this article

Idea Maps at work

A large engineering firm in Seattle wanted to expand their consulting services to include environmental engineering. This expansion involved setting up new departments, adding personnel, and developing a separate division within the corporation. Using the Idea Mapping techniques, they mapped out all work to be done by quarter's end. Additionally, they drafted the contents of a new company brochure.

Even with a major report that requires lots of data, you can still (*with practice*) complete an Idea Map in about ten minutes.

Dr. Julie Tip:
For group writing projects:
1. Circle each major point with different colors to make them easier to identify.
2. Then assign each branch to individual team members.
3. Each team member Idea Maps his or her branch and adds any further data or information necessary to the project.
This works great for business plans and grant or proposal writing—actually any large document.

The training director of a manufacturing company used to pull her hair out when considering a new hire because she spent hours capturing and processing everyone's ideas. She shared this comment: "It would put me over the edge! Now, in a half-hour I can Idea Map the job requirements with my team and have the position posted that afternoon!"

A human resources director said procrastination used to be her middle name when it came to completing performance reviews. To add to the workload, she had to write the monthly reviews for probationary hires. "After drawing up an Idea Map on a Sunday afternoon, I felt much better about taking on this daunting, tedious and time-consuming chore!"

Idea Maps save you time!

Here's her Idea Map. She made a template, or a model, to use for all her reviews, since the same points were addressed about each employee. This kind of template could also be used to set up sales and marketing presentations. Just plug in the topics.

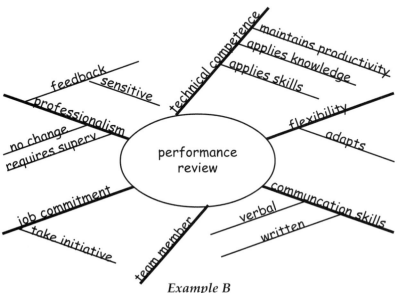

Example B
A template for performance reviews

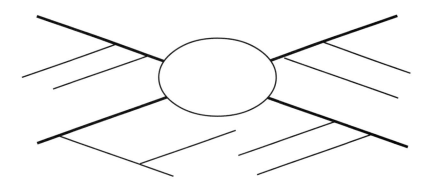 Practice: Create an Idea Map

Apply the steps and create an Idea Map on any topic—perhaps a speech for a conference, a marketing proposal, a response to a customer complaint, or a plan for a product rollout. Try several to practice. After charting six or seven Idea Maps, you will create them effortlessly.

To start, put your main idea in the center below and get going!

If you want more creative/innovative thinking in your organization, you must encourage the generation of "qualities of ideas."
     -Michael Michalko, Cracking Creativity

Four More Ways to Idea Map

Information can be organized in a variety of different ways, depending on the task and the person creating the Idea Map. In the previous examples, the Idea Maps displayed key concepts about the main idea. Four additional ways to organize your thoughts, data, or points onto an Idea Map follow, with examples of each below:

1. Division of information
2. Compare and contrast
3. Cause and effect
4. Problem and solution

Depending on your writing tasks—project proposals, press releases, marketing materials—one of these Idea Map formats probably will work for you. Again, the mapping questions give structure to your ideas.

But *remember:* No matter what format you use, it must stay reader-oriented. Ask yourself: How will I effectively and concisely present my points to the reader?

Now, let's look at some scenarios in which you might use the four different formats mentioned above, along with some pertinent mapping questions.

Division of Information

Dividing information remains probably the most widely used organizational format because of its built-in logic. You can organize the information in one of the following ways:

• Chronological (used for information related to time or historical references)
• Most to least important (used to explain)
• Least to most important (used in persuade)

- Listing steps (used for procedures and instructions)

As you create an Idea Map, consider these examples of mapping questions:

- In what order will we roll out this initiative?
- What problems need addressing as we begin large-scale hiring?
- What steps should be followed in this process?
- What reasons should (or not) be considered when supporting this project?
- What seem to be logical divisions for the presentation of this report/sales proposal?

Scenario: ABC Corporation plans a marketing campaign for a new product launch.
Mapping Question: *What key ideas should we focus on as we take this product to market?*

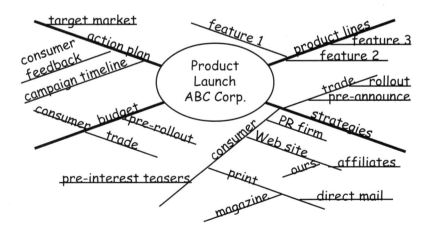

Compare and contrast

In this next approach, you can organize data by contrasting and comparing and/or presenting advantages and disadvantages. For example, perhaps you want to compare the attributes of your product/services versus that of your competitor's.

As you create an Idea Map, consider these examples of mapping questions:

- What familiar ideas can I use to link this new and unfamiliar information so that the team understands?
- How will I compare and/or contrast our product/service to that of our competitors?
- What key issues surround the advantages and disadvantages of starting this project?

Scenario: A bank wants to consider new products that match up with their competitors.

Mapping Question: *What are the differences and similarities between our products/services and those of our competitors?*

Cause and effect

You can also organize your information around a question-answer or cause-and-effect format. This means you would consider various actions and their corresponding results. For example: If we proceed one way, this will happen; if we proceed a different way, that will happen.

As you create an Idea Map, consider these examples of mapping questions:

- What questions might our customers have about this new product?
- What is the cause-and-effect relationship of this product purchase?
- What are the problems and what are the solutions to this issue?

Scenario: A fast-growing company considers the pros and cons of using in-house trainers versus outsourcing.

Mapping Question: *What are the advantages and disadvantages between in-house training and outsourcing?*

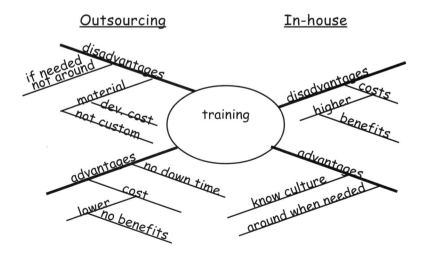

Problem and solution

This last approach has great appeal, since that's what we do for our customers—solve their problems. For example: Here's your problem, here's how we can solve it *and* achieve these results.

As you create an Idea Map, consider these examples of mapping questions:

- What facts, reasoning, and conclusions would reinforce our position?
- What approaches might solve my client's issues?

Scenario: A business must solve its problem of limited parking for employees, which is compounded by the fact that it shares an entrance with a local community college.

Mapping Question: *What are the ways we can solve the problem of not enough parking?*

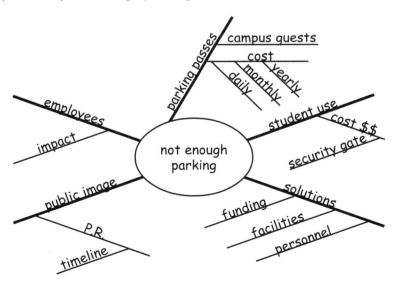

Now you try it

Now it's time for you to chart your own Idea Map. Use existing documents or create ones that you need to get started. For example, how about using one of the Idea Mapping formats to start updating a business plan or create a series of instructions necessary for a database?

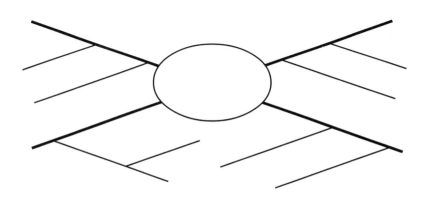

Important: Hold on to your Idea Map. In the next chapter, you'll use it to start your writing.

It is my contention—my superstition if you like—that he who is faithful to his map, and consults it, and draws from it his inspiration, daily and hourly, gains positive support... The tale has a root here: it grows in that soil; it has a spine of its own behind the words...As he studies the map, relations will appear that he had not thought upon.

-Robert Louis Stevenson

Five Reasons to Idea Map

❑ **Pre-planning**: Idea Mapping organizes major projects and reports. It allows for brainstorming and creativity before you begin the work.

❑ **Test preparation**: Idea Mapping arranges lecture notes or chapters in your textbook. It makes it easier to see all the important points on one piece of paper.

A colleague of mine used Idea Mapping to organize her thesis in her MBA program. She said, "There was absolutely no conceivable way to organize all the data and research over three years by using a formal outline. The outline would have been as thick as our course notebooks! Idea Mapping was the only way. I could see virtually the entire paper on one very big piece of butcher paper. It was a miracle!"

❑ **Note-taking at meetings or lectures:** Idea Mapping simplifies getting down the main points covered. No one speaks without *bird walk*s (goes off on a tangent—see definition at end of chapter). You can use Idea Mapping to capture the main ideas even if the speaker is prone to meandering.

❑ **Problem solving**: Idea Mapping gives you permission to think through an issue creatively.

❑ **Project management**: Idea Mapping can help project managers complete statements of work, work breakdown structure, project post-mortem, and status reports.

Singing from the Same Songbook

The following words and phrases will pop up throughout this book. For each one I've given the definition as it pertains to our discussion about writing. Sharing a common vocabulary with your reader is important any time you want to communicate effectively—a point you might want to remember as you work on your own writing.

You may want to put a place holder here for easy reference.

Bird walk ~ Going off on a tangent; important information that needs including but may be slightly off course; an aside.

Concluding Power 1 ~ Sentence or paragraph that seals your document. See Chapter Three.

Free-writing with an edge ~ Using the power numbers as your edge, to get your thoughts written down in an organized manner. See Chapter Two.

Idea Map ~ A graphic representation of your ideas on paper.

Mapping question ~ A focused question about your topic that guides your thinking and brainstorming.

Mnemonic ~ A memory technique. See C.L.E.V.R. Solutions in Chapter Four.

Pedantic writing ~ Writing that no one understands but may impress some readers.

Power Numbering ~ An organizational writing system that assigns a numerical value (a power) to words, phrases, sentences, and paragraphs.

Power 1 ~ The main idea of your document. Used at the beginning and end of a document.

Power 2 ~ The major point(s) about your topic. It explains or supports your main idea. Power 2 always talks about Power 1.

Power 3 ~ A minor point or detail about Power 2. Power 3 always talks about, supports, elaborates on the Power 2. Power 4s and 5s can add even further specifics, as long as each power refers to the preceding power.

Voice ~ Revealing who you are through your writing; your unique way of expressing yourself.

Zero power ~ Sentences that hook the reader or provide background information.

In Summary

Using Idea Maps will:
* Allow you to quickly generate ideas and organize data.
* Free you from the fear and procrastination of getting started.
* Open up your creativity without the mind- numbing outline structure.
* Supply an organizational tool when you already know the topic.
* Let you see your entire writing project at a glance.
* Provide an excellent process for group projects or large reports.
* Help make sense of large amounts of data.
* Organize one-page letters or 1,000-page tomes.

What's Next

In the next chapter, you will:
* Organize your Idea Map into a Power framework.
* Master the Power Numbers system.
* Understand how using the Power Numbers helps you produce clear, crisp communication.
* Convert the Power framework into a draft with Power sentences.
* Practice free-writing that first draft.
* Learn how to keep your writing on target and completed in half the time!

Get ready for the Power Play!

CHAPTER TWO

GET STARTED

Cut Your Writing Time in Half!

In Chapter One, we talked about using Idea Mapping right from the get-go whenever you have to write. A quick way to brain dump, Idea Mapping corrals all those galloping ideas before they can escape out the barn door.

For some of you, this unstructured approach understandably conflicts with your learning style. If that applies to you, not to worry—you can go straight to the Power Numbers. They will give you the framework you need to both generate and organize your ideas, *and* **get started**.

If you can count to three, you can write anything you ever have to in this or any other lifetime!

Remember the Idea Map on *time management habits* in Chapter One? Here it is again, with each branch assigned a Power Number: larger branches represent Power 2s and the twigs are Power 3s and 4s.

Quick—what's the Power Number in the circle?

You got it—Power 1, the topic of the Idea Map.

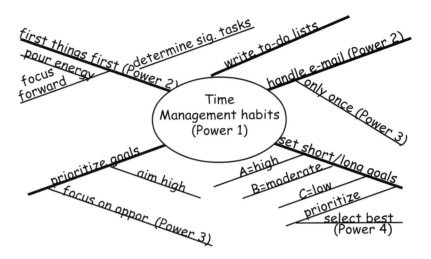

Below I have converted the Idea Map into the Power Numbers structure. (See Chapter One for the Idea Mapping steps):

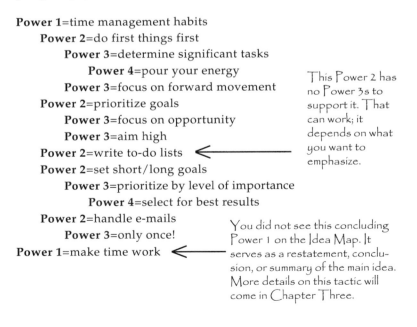

Power 1=time management habits
  Power 2=do first things first
    Power 3=determine significant tasks
      Power 4=pour your energy
    Power 3=focus on forward movement
  Power 2=prioritize goals
    Power 3=focus on opportunity
    Power 3=aim high
  Power 2=write to-do lists ⟵
  Power 2=set short/long goals
    Power 3=prioritize by level of importance
      Power 4=select for best results
  Power 2=handle e-mails
    Power 3=only once!
Power 1=make time work ⟵

This Power 2 has no Power 3s to support it. That can work; it depends on what you want to emphasize.

You did not see this concluding Power 1 on the Idea Map. It serves as a restatement, conclusion, or summary of the main idea. More details on this tactic will come in Chapter Three.

I tell my clients, "If you can count to three, you can write anything you ever have to in this or any other lifetime!"

For those of you who can toggle back and forth between the two organizing tools, you can start with an Idea Map, then convert it into Power Numbers (above), or vice versa.

It is true! I have worked with over half a million people in every imaginable industry—from school districts to software conglomerates to insurance companies—have utilized this system.

People at all levels—from CEOs to trades people to students… in companies of all sizes—from large corporations to small businesses to one-person enterprises…to people who are government employees, hospital administrators, restaurateurs, travel agents, realtors, attorneys, financial planners, and accountants (just to name a few!)—have learned the Power Numbers system and made it work for them.

Everywhere I take this system, great things happen! From saving companies hundreds of thousands of dollars to making people feel empowered, successful, and confident, the **Power Numbers system creates positive results** every time. The people I teach say, "This is so easy! Why didn't I learn this in school? I wouldn't have been so afraid to write." Another frequent comment: "I can't believe how much time this saves! I can easily and rapidly organize my ideas with the Power Numbers!"

A dirty little secret

I'll let you in on a little secret: all informational writing— whether business, research-based, persuasive, technical, or analytical—follows a formula. The writer introduces the main point of his/her document then proceeds to logically unpack the ideas. For example: *Here's the idea, here are major points about it, and here are some specifics to back it up*. In turn, readers look for that clear organization, those key words that lead them to the details that lend evidence of support. Sounds simple, right?

The trouble is we were never taught this formula. We learned abstract terms that English teachers loved—topic sentence/thesis statement, introduction, body, and conclusion. These terms may have meant something, but in most cases they did not conjure up substantive images that helped us write a clear and organized paper.

Use numbers to write

The Power Numbers system uses numbers to give order to your thinking and your writing, allowing you to easily arrange your ideas in a logical sequence. *And,* for those who like the organization outlining provides, this framework gives you the best of both worlds: the structure of an outline, without its creativity-killing rigid rules!

The Power Numbers System

The **Power Numbers system** consists of assigning a numerical value—a Power—to words, phrases, sentences, and paragraphs. The numbers correspond to the level of importance and detail you want in your document. By using the numbers, you can quickly organize your ideas and get writing!

This is so easy! Why haven't I learned it until now?

Numbers are your friends

- **Power 1** is the main theme, topic sentence, topic paragraph, thesis statement, big idea, or focus of your document. It may be the first sentence of your document or be included within the first paragraph. Power 1 can also be used as a concluding sentence, restating your main theme, topic sentence, or big idea. (More details on this will be given in Chapter Three.)

- **Power 2** is a major point or detail about your Power 1. It clarifies, explains, or supports your main theme. Power 2s always talk about Power 1. Power 2s make up the body of your document.

- **Power 3** is a minor point or detail about Power 2. Power 3 always talks about, elaborates upon, or adds specific details about the major points (Power 2s). Add as many Power 3s as you need to back up your major points.

You can add increasing levels of detail to any document of any length. How? By adding Power 4s and Power 5s. In most documents, you will only need Power 2s and 3s to make your point; in others—depending on the purpose—more detail is necessary. Just remember, each number must support or expand on the preceding Power Number.

For those of you who think in pictures, this diagram should help you see the Power Number framework extended out to Power 4s and 5s. See how the Power 1 frames the ideas that follow.

Let's get back to business

Now that we've looked at an overview of the numbering system, I'll show you how to build any document of any length.

Look at a simple paragraph with each sentence defined as a Power 1, 2, or 3:

Follow these three steps for turning on your computer (Power 1). First, be sure you plug it in (Power 2). Purchase a power-surge cord to insure against future problems (Power 3). Second, press in the button on your PC tower (Power 2). You will hear a whirring sound; this is the computer starting (Power 3). Last, press the button on your monitor (Power 2). Your monitor will spring to life with color and graphics (Power 3)!

> The Power 1 states the topic; the Power 2s support the main idea; the Power 3s provide the details.

Start *first* with Power 1s and Power 2s

Okay, time to build your own document with Power Numbers. Let's do a practice run first.

To start, use Power 1 and Power 2 **words and phrases** to capture your thoughts. Later you will expand them into sentences.

Let's look at a few examples. In the first, the Power 1 is *product offerings* (the main theme) and the Power 2s are the *names of the products* (the major points).

> Power 1=product/service offerings
> >Power 2=consulting
> >Power 2=specialized electronic dictionaries
> >Power 2=voice recognition software

How about this example:

Power 1=improving employee morale
Power 2=performance-driven bonuses
Power 2=flexible work hours
Power 2=college tuition reimbursement

And here's one more:

Power 1=financial institutions
Power 2=Washington Mutual Bank
Power 2=U.S. Bank
Power 2=Umpqua Bank
Power 2=Commerce Bank

Can you see the core of each writer's document beginning to take shape?

Practice: Start with Power 1 and 2s

How many major points (Power 2s) will clarify or explain a new program to your employees or to your customers? List your Power 2 ideas in words and phrases in the blanks below.

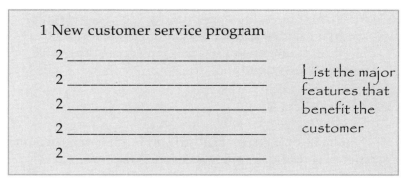

1 New customer service program

2 _____

2 _____   List the major features that

2 _____   benefit the

2 _____   customer

2 _____

Or perhaps you need to get out a memo informing your staff about a change in the organization. What three reasons would you share with staff about the sales team reconfiguration?

1 Changes in the sales team

2 _____

2 _____

2 _____

Build your document with words and phrases

The steps

1 **Find your Idea Map** from Chapter One. Now take out a piece of paper or go to your PC and get ready to write down a Power 1 followed by Power 2s.

2 **Write down the Power 1**—the main theme of your document. This would be the circled word or phrase in the middle of your Idea Map. (See page 21.)

3 **Count each branch**—those lines radiating from the circle. That number determines how many Power 2s you will list. (In my Idea Map, I have five branches; therefore, five Power 2s list the time management habits.) For further guidance see the Appendix.

Add Power 3s

Now let's branch out a bit. To add more details or some specifics about your topic, you need **Power 3s**.

In the example below, the Power 3s elaborate about employee morale. The Power 3s list specific outcomes derived from boosting morale.

Example:

Power 1=improving employee morale
Power 2=performance-driven bonuses
Power3=instills pride and ownership
Power 2=flexible work hours
Power 3=builds sense of trust
Power 2=college tuition reimbursement
Power 3=empowers employees

Here's another example:

Power 1=New customer service program
Power 2=Increase customer loyalty
Power 3=greet each customer

Build your   Power 3=mail thank you notes
document   Power 2=Feel free to make decisions
with Power   Power 3=waive fees
Numbers   Power 3=offer products
Power 2=one-stop services
Power 3=online bill pay
Power 3=credit cards
Power 3=mortgages
Power 2=help from bank staff

Dr Julie Tip:
You can add as many Power 2s and 3s as you want to make any point of any length.

---

4 **Look over your Idea Map again.** The Power 3s, 4s, and 5s are the twigs on your Idea Map. Add these minor points about the topic to your Power structure.

Power 3s are great for giving additional information, but don't feel you always have to put them in whatever you're writing. Some Power 2s require additional elaboration, others do not.

The Power Numbers can expand with any document to any length—you decide. Just remember you always build your writing around the needs of your reader and your purpose for writing.

Let's Get Writing and Start Counting!

Congratulations! You've made it over the initial hurdles: You've organized by charting an Idea Map (or two). You've started by using the Power Numbers. Now, you can begin writing sentences.

At this point, you don't want to waste time trying to construct an introduction or beginning that will knock the reader's socks off. That comes later. Right now you want to just jump right in and **write the Power 1 sentence.** Simple is best to start. You'll come back later and revise.

In the next section you'll take your Power words and phrases and turn them into clear, crisp, concise memos, e-mails, letters, reports, proposals—anything you need to write. By using the Power Numbers system, you save time. Knowing how many points you will write about in your document cuts your organizing and writing time in half. Best of all, you will deliver **writing worth reading.**

Power phrases converted into power sentences

Below I have turned Power 1 and 2 words and phrases from page 28 into sentences on *time management habits.* Remember, these sentences are in draft form.

Time Management Habits

Power 1=Practicing five indispensable habits is your passbook to a full and rich life.
Power 2=Do first things first.
Power 2=Prioritizing your goals is the second habit.

Power 2=A third habit consists of writing to-do lists.
Power 2=Set short- and long-range goals.
Power 2=Learn how to handle the slew of e-mails that arrive each day.
Power 1=Make time work.

Before you draft your Power 1 and 2 sentences, read on.

Free-Write, but with Restraint

Does that sound like an oxymoron? Free-writing conjures up images of blithely dumping down on paper whatever darn thing comes to mind, then spending excessive amounts of time going back to organize those chaotic thoughts.

But with the Power Numbers system, you can free-write and organize at the same time. Here's how: As you let those sentences flow, use the Power Numbers to assign their level of importance, thus creating some semblance of order while saving time!

Never correct or rewrite until the whole thing is down. Rewrite in process is usually found to be an excuse for not going on.
—John Steinbeck

Worry-free free writing

Your internal editor may be itching to use his red pen, but tell him to keep a cap on it for now. Just get your sentences down without undue attention to punctuation, spelling, and the other writing rules—you'll go back later in the process to make sure everything is correct.

By using the Power Numbers you have control so that you stay focused and don't wander. The Power Numbers act as guides so that less time (and money) will be spent later reorganizing the material.

Remember, a draft is just that—a first attempt. Just like building a house, a draft lays the foundation for you to build upon and produce a great written document.

Spend your very valuable time *after* you shape your document. Similar to putting a jigsaw puzzle together, the fun lies in seeing the pieces fall into place. The parts become whole and form a clear picture, the one intended by the designer. (We'll talk further about the rewriting process in Chapter Three.)

Dr. Julie Tip:

For writing this draft:

- Use whatever writing tool works for you. Some people can compose directly on the computer; others find writing in long-hand more comfortable.
- Keep in mind that no one will read this first draft.
- Tell yourself that, although writing is a necessary and sometimes daunting chore, you'll get through it.
- Give yourself a time limit, approximately twenty to thirty minutes, to just get your thoughts down. Take a break, and then come back and reread what you wrote. It will help you get started again. But do not spend time revising yet.
- Recognize that this draft is rough, messy, and undisciplined. That's okay. Just let go and write. Mastering this important technique will help your writing tremendously.

You're in good company

Everyone writes that dreaded first draft—even good writers! In *Bird by Bird,* author Anne Lamott describes her writing of first drafts: "I'd write a first draft that was maybe twice as long as it should be, with a self-indulgent and boring beginning, stupefying descriptions… lots of quotes from my black-humored friends… and no ending to speak of. The whole thing would be so long and incoherent and hideous that for the rest of the day I'd obsess about getting creamed by a car before I could write a decent second draft."

> *… perfectionism will ruin your writing, blocking inventiveness and playfulness and life force (these words we are allowed to use in California). Perfectionism means that you try desperately not to leave so much mess to clean up.*
>
> -Anne Lamott

Prolific author Peter DeVries confessed, "I love being a writer. What I can't stand is the paperwork!" In a more serious vein, James Michener was often quoted as saying that he wasn't a great writer, but the world's best re-writer. Another writer stated: "Like many writers, I don't like to write; I like to have written."

As you can see, when you write a draft, you're in good company. Writing that first draft will lead you to your final masterpiece!

Remember: Don't give in to the temptation to rewrite each phrase or sentence. Trying to get it perfect at this point will only block the flow of your ideas, slow you down, and waste time! Just keep moving—you can come back and tidy up later.

✒️ Practice: Write Power sentences

Use the following strategy to get writing **Power sentences!**

1 Start by counting the number of Power 2s from your Power structure (see page 34). Those are your major points.

2 Now, write your Power 1 (topic) sentence, mentioning the number of points you plan to write about.

Approach this process as if you were writing the *Cliff's Notes* of your final product.

For example, you might have *five* components to the customer service program or *three* reasons for changes in the sales department. By putting that number in the Power 1 sentence, you quickly create an organizational mindset and give yourself permission to just start writing.

You know where you're going, you know how many points you're going to write about, and guess what? So does the reader! You'll see what I'm talking about in the examples below.

The following are Power 1 sentences include a number to guide the reader:

- *Three* charming cities in Europe should not be missed!
- Our new customer service plan offers *five* money-saving ideas.
- Due to product sales decline, our sales department must undergo *three* personnel changes.

- In this era of expanding education rhetoric but restrained state spending, it's useful to compare *two* ideas.
    The Seattle Times
- Contemporary politics has *three* peculiarities.
    The Washington Post
- The administration faced a *two*-front war.
    Los Angeles Times

You will save your readers time with this strategy. They can skim your paper by reading just the major points.

Once again, looking at the *time management* example, the Power 1 sentence could read: *Practicing five indispensable time management habits can be your passbook to a full and rich life.*

3 Continue to build your document by converting your Power 2s and 3s into complete sentences. Work your way down the Power structure. You might want to write your Power 2 sentences **first** and then go back and add your Power 3s.

A bird walk: Putting a number in the Power 1 sentence is not an absolute! But it jump-starts your writing. For example, the Power 1 sentence for the *time management* article could be written: *Learning important time management habits can be your passbook to a full and rich life.*

The following Power 1 sentences *do not* have a number to guide the reader:

- Rhode Island and Pennsylvania illustrate the spectrum of economic development activity.
    Insight

- Necessary changes to the sales department will increase our revenue this next quarter.
- Our new customer service program keeps us competitive.
- While traveling in Europe, don't miss visiting these charming cities.

You decide whether your sentence needs that introductory number or not. Your decision will depend on:

- ❑ the document length
- ❑ the purpose of the document
- ❑ your good judgment about what your reader needs

Power sentences converted into paragraphs

It's time to take those simple sentences and **expand them into paragraphs**. To do that means you want to look at your document as a whole.

First, let's just review the way the Power Numbers system works. When you started with your Idea Map, you had words or phrases to which you assigned Power Numbers: Your Power 1 phrase was supported by your Power 2 phrases, which were supported by your Power 3s.

Next you converted those phrases into sentences, again with Power 3 sentences elaborating on Power 2s, which in turn spoke about the Power 1.

As you can see, whether you use words, phrases, or sentences, the structure remains the same: the larger the Power Number, the more detailed your writing becomes.

When you construct your document, you will apply the same Power Numbering system to the paragraphs within your document. Each paragraph will have a Power of its own as it relates to the other paragraphs. At this point, you probably don't need to apply a Power Number to individual sentences within the paragraph. Instead, look at the bigger picture— meaning make sure that each paragraph supports the paragraph it should.

Here's an example of what a document might look like if you assigned Power Numbers to the paragraphs:

Introduction
Paragraph 1   Power 1(Main idea)

Body
Paragraph 2   Power 2
                 supports Paragraph 1
                 (Power 1-Main Idea)
Paragraph 3   Power 2
                 supports Paragraph 1
                 (Power 1-Main idea)
Paragraph 4   Power 3
                 supports Paragraph 3
                 (Power 2-Major point)
Paragraph 5   Power 4
                 supports Paragraph 4
                 (Power 3-Minor point)
Paragraph 6   Power 2
                 supports Paragraph 1
                 (Power 1-Main idea)

Conclusion
Paragraph 7   Power 1
                 wraps up document
(More about this ending in Chapter Three.)

Even though the Power 2 paragraphs may have Power 3 sentences within them, the paragraph as a whole supports the Power 1. If you've followed the exercises, and practiced the Power Numbering system, this kind of logical sequencing will come naturally, whether you're working with words, phrases, sentences, or paragraphs.

Time Management article with Power 2 paragraphs

Practicing five indispensable time management habits can be your passbook to a full and rich life.

This is a Power 1 paragraph—it states the topic. See Chapter Three for tips on writing introductory paragraphs.

Start by focusing on first things first. By determining the most significant work for you to accomplish, you narrow your concentration to a few activities that get results. Since not enough time is available to do everything, choose the most important tasks and pour your energy into those.

Power 2 paragraph describes the first habit.

Second, prioritize your goals. Your goals must be centered around opportunities rather than past failures. Only through ranking your objectives will you achieve focus.

Power 2 paragraph describes the second habit.

A third habit consists of writing to-do lists. Goal-oriented people always write things down. By doing so, goals become more than just ideas. Writing makes them real.

Power 2 paragraph describes the third habit.

Fourth, setting short- and long-range goals should become an ingrained habit. This process consists of deciding what level of importance each of them has. Then organize the tasks around completing your goals.

Power 2 paragraph describes the fourth habit.

Last, learning how to handle the slew of e-mails that arrive each day is imperative. Touching the same message more than once wastes an inordinate amount of time.

Power 2 paragraph describes the fifth habit.

Making time work for you—— A Power 1 sentence
remains the most important habit *you*   concludes the article.
can acquire in today's extraordinarily   See Chapter Three for
busy world.   techniques on writing
                                          concluding paragraphs.

Now you try it

Build your sentences into Power paragraphs. Convert
your Power 2 sentences into separate *Power*graphs.

Practice: Expand into multi-paragraph documents

The *time management* article below is expanded into Power
3 paragraphs. Just as the whole of the Power 2 paragraph supports the Power 1 (the main idea) in your document, so do the
Power 3 paragraphs support the Power 2 paragraph by adding specifics, data, or perhaps rationale. See example below.

The Power 3 paragraphs expand the *time management*
habits example.

Expanded Time Management article with Power 3 paragraphs

Practicing five indispensable time
management habits can be your passbook to a full and rich life.

Start by focusing on first things first.
By determining the most significant
work for you to accomplish, you narrow
your concentration to a few activities that
get results. Since not enough time is available to do everything, choose the most
significant tasks and pour your energy
into those.

Repeating this daily mantra—I must do *first things first*—forces you to hone in on important work and eliminate those tasks that don't move you forward.

Power 3 paragraph clarifies what it means to do first things first.

Second, prioritize your goals. They must be centered on opportunities rather than past failures. Only through ranking your objectives will you achieve focus.

Focusing on future opportunities should drive the organization. You can't change what's happened, you can only prepare for what will happen. That's where your energy and attention must be directed—outward towards success. Remember to always aim high!

Power 3 paragraph explains why the reader should focus on opportunities.

A third habit consists of writing to-do lists. Goal-oriented people always write things down. By doing so, goals become more than just ideas. Writing goals down makes them real, concrete, and attainable.

No Power 3 paragraph was needed here.

Fourth, setting short- and long-range goals should become an ingrained habit. This process consists of deciding what level of importance each goal has. Then organize your tasks around completing the goals.

Label these tasks A, B, and C. *A* tasks always get picked, as they will create results. Those tasks labeled **B** are placed in a file that says "pending," while the **C** tasks are put in a drawer that may read "when hell freezes over." Translation: No time or energy should be spent on **C** tasks.

Power 3 paragraph gives the reader specific tips for labeling tasks.

Last, learning how to handle the slew of e-mails that arrives each day is imperative. Touching the same message more than once wastes an inordinate amount of time.

It would stagger the imagination to consider how many times you review the same e-mail before you act on it. Force yourself to make a decision about each piece of correspondence *the first time*. Will you file it, delete it, or respond to it? Choose.

Power 3 paragraph details e-mail handling.

Anyone can acquire these five habits. Simple, tested, and proven in the real world of work, they help you accomplish more—in less time, thus freeing you for enjoyable pursuits. Making time work for you remains the most important habit you can acquire in today's extraordinarily busy world.

Expanded paragraph=concluding Power 1 paragraph.

Now you try it

Expand your draft. Add Power 3 paragraphs. These paragraphs elaborate on your Power 2 ideas. Specifically, Power 3s clarify main points by providing examples, defining terms or offering clear explanations.

Count backwards

If you read the paragraphs above in reverse, you find that the Power 3 paragraph supports the major point contained in the previous Power 2 paragraph. The Power 2 paragraphs speak to the Power 1.

Go back up the Power sentences in your draft and check whether they follow a logical sequence. This will assure you that you stayed focused and organized.

*Power*ful short stories

One of the great joys in my work comes when clients share success stories about how the Power Numbers system has worked for them. An assistant director of a large county agency told me "Precision is a nonnegotiable" in her office. "Mistakes in communication cost millions of government dollars. Using the Power Numbers to organize our complicated policy and procedure manuals was a lifesaver! The manuals were just plain simpler to read."

A United Way director said, "Learning the Power Numbers was easy. I have a logical mind, so the numbers just made sense. It's an informal outline approach that makes my writing that much more efficient."

A different response came from my friend, a well-known national radio and TV announcer of the financial news. "I tend to be very global and random in my thinking process. So, my speaking can sometimes be all over the map. The Power Numbers help me stay organized in this incredibly warp-speed job. I use the numbers to clarify issues for my listeners. For example, the three key points in the new tax law, or the five important ideas that Dr. Ben Bernanke stated in his last pronouncement; or the one essential component to 'playing the market.'"

> *Good writing is writing that works. It makes sense. It's both comfy and elegant. It says just enough and no more. It has manners, not mannerisms. Good writing has all the right words— and not too many of them—in all the right places.*
> *-Patricia T. O'Conner*

A highly regarded software company that creates programs for graphic artists uses the numbering system with its development team. "The numbers guide the conceptual flow for our products. This is the key we were missing!"

Nowhere is reducing writing time more crucial than in the tech world. IT project managers are on the fast track, running at double time with the tasks increasing *ad infini-tum*. The project manager of a truck manufacturing company said, "The numbering system gave us the framework for documenting our plan. We saved an amazing amount of time completing these complicated work plans!"

The Power Numbers system works because:

- **The Power Numbers are concrete and logical.** The numbers organize your thinking, your writing, even your speaking.

- **With the Power Numbers, you control your writing by using however many Power Numbers you need to make the points you want.** You don't get locked into following any prescribed outline format that slows you down and takes time. Your writing organizes around what makes sense.

- **The Power Numbers contribute one of the key ingredients to good, effective writing—organization.** Without it your reader is lost and so is your message.

Use Power Numbers to clear up these problems:

- **Organization:** The numbers make it easy for the reader to follow your thoughts.

- **Sequencing:** The numbers point the way.

- **Supporting details, examples, or anecdotes:** The Power 3s, 4s, and 5s help make your case.

- **Gaps in information:** Ask yourself: Do the details (Power 3s) directly relate to what was stated in Power 2? Do the Power 2s really support the idea presented in your Power 1 sentence? Check and see. The numbers give you a *reality check* on how well you organized your document.

Practice: Review your document

Check over your paragraphs. Do you have:
- ❑ Power 3s that really talk about the preceding Power 2?
- ❑ Power 2s that unpack the main idea presented in the Power 1?
- ❑ A document that accomplishes what you want?
- ❑ Enough information for your reader to know what to do with the message?

Test your skills

Now it's time to see what you know. You've written using the Power Numbers. Now let's look at other people's writing. The benefit? Learn to step back and view your writing. See how well organized you are.

Identify the organizational structure by determining the *Power* (*1, 2, 3,* or *4*) of each sentence in these paragraphs. (Answers in Appendix.)

1 There are *two* Seattles on prime-time television. One is rendered by *Millennium*, the Friday-night creep show...The result is a depressing hour of television... The other Seattle of TV Land is a damned site more cheerful. *Frasier*, the hit sitcom on NBC, is ensconced in a stunning, immaculate Queen

The transition words—*one . . . the other*—serve to guide the reader.

Anne apartment overlooking the Space Needle and downtown.

Pacific Northwest Magazine

2 Egypt offers *six* advantages to American investment. It has a unique location with access to
European, African, and Arab markets. It has the
broadest industrial base in
the Arab world. It has a
large cadre of industrially
skilled workers. It has a
system of advanced voca-
tional education centers
that offer training custom-
made to an investor's labor
needs. It has investment
laws that provide profit
and capital repatriation privileges, and even
more special advantages for firms operating in
free zones. It has an eagerness to acquire and
apply Western technology.

No obvious transition
words (like those above)
are used in this paragraph.
But you can easily follow
the six points by the
writer's repetitive use of the
words "it has."

Nation's Business

3 Why do people who
fight against cancer do
better than those who
do not fight? For one
reason, fighters take
better care of them-
selves. A fighter gets
out of bed earlier and walks, even with painful
incisions. A nonfighter doesn't and gets an infec-
tion in his/her lungs. A prime reason that fighters do better, though, comes from the physiologi-
cal. Psychoneuroimmunology researchers have
solid evidence that emotions, mental attitudes, and
coping all strongly affect the immune system.

While the first two
examples used a number in
the Power 1 sentence, this
paragraph uses transitions
to walk the reader through
the points.

Reader's Digest

4 Two stories illustrate the American way of thinking about entrepreneurship. The first relates the story of the entrepreneurial hero—the plucky individual who uses energy, effort, daring, and good luck to rise in the world. This character, found in every story written by Horatio Alger, has received celebrity status throughout American history; and people still admire him today. His story, though, has an unhappy ending. The second story holds more promise. It focuses not on the individual but on the team. One example lies in Tracy Kidder's *The Soul of a New Machine,* a book that describes how a group of engineers pooled their talents to design a new computer.

Can you find the Power 4?

Harvard Business Review

All informational writing follows a basic organizational structure. Ideas are logically presented to the reader, then supported and defended through additional argumentation, recommendations, or data.

The reader looks for that structure. If the reader has to work too hard, you have erred in your ways. Use the numbers to keep your writing simple, direct, and well organized.

In Summary

The Power Numbers system, elegant in its simplicity, works because it:
- Gets you started.
- Gives you a shortcut.
- Saves you time and, therefore, money.
- Helps you organize.
- Results in lean writing; lean writing gets read!
- Stops you from circling the computer.
- Helps you produce more powerful documents.

In Chapter Two you learned how these numbers not only keep you and the reader on track but can also cut your writing time in half.

What's Next

In the next chapter, you will:
- Practice writing beginnings and endings.
- Understand how transitions smooth out style.
- Break another rule.
- Realize the importance of writing like you talk.
- Review, revise, refine your draft.
- Learn how much fun this process is.
- Review Dr. Julie's Guiding Principles.
- Produce a document worth reading.

Now comes the fun part!

Chapter Three

Get It Done

Review, Revise, Refine

Chapter Two lets you in on a secret good business writers already know: the best way to engage your reader is by delivering information in a clear, logical order. To do that, good writers construct their documents with sentences that refer to or build on preceding sentences.

Some people know how to do this intuitively. For those of us who don't, all we have to do is follow the Power Numbers system. As you saw in Chapter Two, this simple method guides you toward building your document by organizing your ideas—step by step, sentence by sentence, paragraph by paragraph.

So far you've learned how to get organized with Idea Maps and get started with Power Numbers. Now it's time **to get it done** by putting on those final but important finishing touches—the opening and closing to your document. This chapter will show you how to create introductions that make your reader sit up and take notice and conclusions that snap your document shut. You will also begin the most important part of the writing process: the revising.

Writing is an art.
Rewriting a craft.
-Marshall Cook

Beginnings
Don't Start By Clearing Your Throat

In this remote-control world, engaging your audience while being brief remains crucial. Readers decide in about three seconds (and I'm being generous!) whether they'll stay with you. Because your reader is likely fighting information overload, your writing has to be heard above the white noise. Those first sentences count!

Are you writing to sell a product, apologize to a customer, summarize a report, persuade someone to change an opinion? Different types of documents require slightly different approaches. Some need a beginning that captures interest right away; others may be more effective if they begin with a personal note; still others should start with essential background information. The purpose of your document will determine which approach you choose.

What you need to know

Before you write that all-important introduction, answer the following questions about your document.

❡ What **type of document are you writing?** Is it:
- ❑ a sales letter?
- ❑ a response to a query or complaint?
- ❑ a follow-up letter?
- ❑ the beginning of an annual report or brochure?
- ❑ an abstract?
- ❑ a cover letter for a job application?

Each of these documents require a different kind of opening.

2 **What is the tone of your document?** To find out, take your *powerful* draft and read through it, preferably aloud. Is the tone:

- professional and businesslike?
- precise and formal?
- informal and conversational?

Both the type of document and the targeted audience will determine the tone you want to use. Striking the right tone is so important because it influences how the reader will react to your message. A document's tone conveys your attitude toward both your subject and your reader and can even establish your organization's personality.

Which of these examples would appeal to *your* reader?

We forthwith acknowledge the receipt of your letter of June 30. Your concern will be taken under consideration.

or

Thank you for sharing your concern about the missing part in your recent order. We will take care of this immediately and are sorry you experienced any inconvenience. Please provide the following information . . .

3 **Who is your reader?** Review these categories to help you determine for whom you are writing your document.

Knowledge Level: What does the reader already know about the topic? Would the reader have questions you can anticipate? How much background information does the reader need to make a decision? Or will the reader pass it up the chain of command?

Relationship: What is your connection with the reader? Direct report? Peer? Supervisor? Potential client?

Personality: What kind of qualities and traits does the reader have? Does your reader prefer facts with ample data or a more informal tone? Does the reader understand and enjoy reading words and phrases such as "heuristics" or "interoperable intermodal transport systems"? Or would a simpler style work better?

You want to write your document to fit your reader's needs. To do that, you need to know about the reader or target audience and how they will perceive your message.

4. **What do you want your document to accomplish?** Knowing **the why** of your message will get you results. Ask yourself the following:

My **purpose** is___(What?)___ so that my reader will do___(What?)___.

Example: My purpose is _to explain my contribution to this company_ so that my reader will _give me a promotion_.

Starting Power

With these answers in hand, you're ready to move on to Zero Power sentences!

Zero Power sentences open a document with a bang. They create interest. They hint at what's coming next. They catch the reader's attention.

This technique of hooking your reader is used all the time in speaking. In writing, Zero Power sentences can be used the same way.

Sales letters, marketing brochures, Web sites, executive summaries for investors, annual reports—all these need beginnings that capture your audience immediately.

You may use as many Zero Power sentences as you need in your opening paragraph to help introduce your topic. However, you still need one—and only one—sentence in the introduction to be your topic sentence—the Power 1 sentence. (See page 60 for an example.) The rest of the beginning sentences build interest, create excitement, provide background data (usually for business cases, proposals, or reports), or even just schmooze with the reader.

- Zero Power sentences ask a question:
  Can the tax code be cut to a paragraph?

- Zero Power sentences state a startling statistic or fascinating fact:
  Chances are greater that you will be run over by a car in your neighborhood than die in a plane crash.

- Zero Power sentences alert the reader to important information contained in the document:
  You've just won the car of your dreams! Read on for details.

- Zero Power sentences can begin with an incident, illustration, or anecdote:
  I toured the city last night in the back of a police car. The close relationship between juvenile delinquency and lack of recreational facilities for teenagers hit me square between the eyes.

- Zero Power sentences can begin with a quote:
  Thomas Edison's definition for genius has often been quoted: "Genius is one percent inspiration and ninety-nine percent perspiration."

- Zero Power sentences can begin with humorous thought (in this case also a famous quote):
  Fewer things are harder to put up with than the annoyance of a good example.
  Mark Twain

Here are some examples from print:

A direct mail letter:

Does your firm lose income because your attorneys do not bill all their time? Our clients have experienced up to a 30 percent increase in billing revenue with our Timekeeper software.

Another mailer:

Steroids for Small Business! Pump up your business with high-speed DSL Internet service from... Free setup, free installation, free equipment.

From Getty Images:

With more than 60 million photographs and 27,000 hours of film from proven brand leaders such as PhotoDisc, The Image Bank and Art.com, Getty Images is the ultimate source for imaging needs.

Let's review the Zero Power sentences that have been added to the *time management* newsletter article in Chapter Two. The Zero Power sentences lead up to the Power 1 sentence* and combine to make an introductory paragraph— a Power 1 paragraph.

Imagine a bank that makes an $86,400 deposit daily into your account, but with a slight hitch—the balance does not carry over and the account returns to zero every night. Time is the same way: You have 86,400 seconds daily to spend any way you wish. They, too, do not carry over to the next day. How you manage those all-too-precious seconds and minutes will determine the quality of your life. *Practicing five indispensable time management habits can be your passbook to a full and rich life.*

✍️ Practice: Write Zero Power sentences

Take any of the following topics and use any of the Zero Power approaches above to write Zero Power sentences for these topics. Here's one example to get you started.

1. A sales pitch for a new product

> *Dear Dr. Julie Miller,*
> *More and more business owners are learning that the Internet is a very powerful tool. We at American Express Small Business Services are taking strides to harness the power of the Web and leverage it for our customers. The Small Business Exchange offers a wealth of information and professional advice that is sure to help you start, grow, and manage your business.*

Two Zero Power sentences and then the Power 1

2. A letter to your local representative favoring action on some legislation
3. A notice informing your clients you are moving your office
4. A proposal for the purchase of new telecommunications equipment
5. The opening comments to a business plan

Dr. Julie Tip:
Want your e-mail to get read? Try putting a Zero Power phrase in the subject line, but also summarizes your message.

Zero Power sentences:
- are usually included in your introductory (Power 1) paragraph.
- add punch to your writing.
- introduce your topic, product, or idea.
- provide necessary background information before launching into points.
- alert the reader to important aspects of your report.
- show warmth as well as relevance of information.
- can stand alone or be integrated into your paragraph.
- can greet or thank your reader.
- may require that you revise your Power 1 sentence so that the two sentences—Zero Power and Power 1—flow together.

I always write a good first line, but I have trouble writing the others.

–Molière

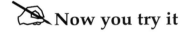

Now you try it

Add Zero Power sentences to the first paragraph of your Chapter Two draft.

Other suggestions for great beginnings

Eliminate tired and hackneyed openings such as:

- Per your request
- Enclosed please find
- Please plan to attend
- Please be advised that
- Regarding our recent conversation
- This is in reference to
- The purpose of this memo is to

Your first sentence counts. These phrases don't grip the reader. Instead, try making your openings more specific. For example, try these:

You requested information about...

or

I have enclosed the information that we discussed...

or

Will you please review the enclosed information...

2 **Build rapport with your reader right away.** You want your words to be meaningful to the reader. A letter that begins:

*We at Emcorp are taking strides to harness the power of the Web...*isn't very exciting. But by adding
...so that you can gain competitive advantage....

you describe a benefit, which makes the reader sit up and take notice.

Dr. Julie Tip:
Check your document for reader benefits.

1. Get out two highlighter pens of different colors.

2. Go through your document, highlighting every time you read about the company's features with one color.

3. Go through the document a second time with the second highlighter. Every time you read about a benefit for your customer, highlight it.

4. Count the number of times you used each highlighter. If the benefits don't outweigh the features, rewrite your document so they do.

Consider this reader-focused benefit in an Avis mailer. I bet you'll open the brochure with these words on the cover!

Avis is trying harder for Mileage Plan members with a free day for you.

3 **Use the words *"you"* or *"your"* within the first two sentences to create a bond between you and the reader.**

This came with my phone bill:

Dear Valued Customer:
Loyalty seems to be a rare commodity these days, particularly when it comes to long distance phone companies. That's why we're pleased by your continued…

Here's an example from a small-business newsletter:

Have you ever had a great idea, an idea so powerful you knew it couldn't miss, but you were unable to find the money to launch your idea? Frustrating, isn't it?

Dr. Julie Tip:
Unless you are creating a technical report, most documents you write will contain a Zero Power sentence. Even letters of rejection have one buffer statement. Did you ever receive a "Dear John" letter after applying for a job? If it read something like this:

You were part of a large pool of outstanding candidates. However…

you were let down easy by that opening Zero Power sentence!

Nothing is wrong with starting off by thanking your reader. Just try to add something personal and specific:

Thank you for sharing the market research with us this week! Your efforts will surely help in securing our second round of financing.

! *As you pull together your Zero Power and Power 1 sentences, you may have to rework the sentences to form a smooth, easy-to-read introductory paragraph.*

Let's see what you know. Review the paragraph below.

✑ Test your skills

Identify the organizational structure by determining the *Power (0, 1, 2, 3, or 4)* of each sentence in this paragraph. (Answer in Appendix.)

Pardon the cynicism, but is the sport ready to rid itself of thugs and thieves? The obvious answer is no, but the iron jaws of Iron Mike could be the starting point for prying the sport away from its jackal promoters. For boxing to survive the laughter, it must reform. First, forbid Mike Tyson from boxing in a sanctioned bout for the rest of his life. Second, fine the promoter. A sport that draws its leading figures from the penitentiaries and rewards them with millions of dollars can't be governed from within. Third, adopt Olympic boxing standards. Tyson couldn't have gotten his teeth into Holyfield if both were wearing regulation-boxing headgear.

The Seattle Times

The Body: Make It Engaging!

The body of your document unpacks the information for the reader. Power 2 and perhaps Power 3 paragraphs comprise the middle section of your document along with transitions to guide the reader.

Depending on your purpose, the body may contain:
- technical data to prove your point.
- methods described for carrying out a project.
- details explaining why your approach is the best one.
- budget details that show costs and justification for those costs.
- personnel qualifications.
- results expected.
- evidence to persuade the reader.
- facts that support the topic.

Now you try it

Check out your draft and see how it shapes up. Do the body paragraphs clearly address your Power 1 idea? Are they in the best order for your document? Have you anticipated your readers' questions and concerns and provided enough examples and explanations to be clear?

Endings
Bring Your Document Full Circle

A Power 1 sentence or paragraph at the end of your document remains just as important as the one that begins it. In fact, the two should work well together to give your documents a smooth finish.

The poet William Yeats wrote about the sound of a finished poem. He described the noise as being like the click of a lid as it closed on a perfectly made box. That same

image applies to a **concluding Power 1 sentence** or paragraph. The document ought to end smoothly, clicking shut
as you logically drive home
your points. Your ending can
determine what remains in
your reader's mind after s/he
has finished reading.

*I always wanted to
write a book that
ended with the word
mayonnaise.*
-Richard Brautigan

You can use many tech-
niques in the concluding
Power 1 sentence or para-
graph, such as providing a
memorable quote, a powerful piece of evidence, or a rhe-
torical question; requesting an action; summarizing your
points; and discussing benefits. Again, the purpose of your
document and your introduction can help determine which
approach you choose.

Concluding Power 1 sentences and paragraphs can:

- Summarize your points to make sure your reader
  has stayed the course:

  *My suggestion is to read the proxy statement when it
  arrives to learn more about the company you own. When
  you are requesting information to study a company, ask
  for the proxy statement along with the annual report. It
  can be very revealing.*

  Better Investing

- Restate or emphasize the main points without repeating the exact words that were already written:

  *Since then, from Korea to Vietnam to the Gulf War,
  Latino families have proudly given their best and
  brightest young people to the service of this country.*

  Los Angeles Times

- Add a different twist or perspective:

  These kids were brought up in a culture of violence, of denial of beauty, yet one kid says, "There's this spray of bullet holes over my door and it looks like a peacock's tail." ...This astonishing image epitomizes poetry for me.

  USC Trojan Family Magazine

- Leave the reader thinking or questioning:

  Wake up, California, or risk being the state that gives new meaning to the phrase, a dim light bulb.

  The Wall Street Journal

- Ask for action from the reader:

  So what are you waiting for?

  Food and Wine

- Let the reader know what happens next:

  If I don't hear from you by Thursday afternoon, I will call you to talk about next steps.

The Power 1 paragraph represents the Power 1 idea, whether it's at the beginning of the document or at the end. Here is the concluding Power 1 paragraph in the *time management* newsletter article, the sentences are combined to make up the conclusion:

Anyone can acquire these five habits. Simple, tested, and proven in the real world of work, they can help you accomplish more in less time, thus freeing you for more enjoyable pursuits. Making time work for you remains the most important habit you can acquire in today's extraordinarily busy world.

This ending brings our article full circle and works well with the opening paragraph. (See Appendix for the full article.)

! *The type, length, or strategy of your document will determine whether you want a concluding* Power 1 *sentence or paragraph. Use the chart below as a useful tool.*

Power Guide

A concluding Power 1 sentence or paragraph is important in:

Application Letters   To request an interview

Reports   To make recommendations, state findings, etc.

Proposals   To reaffirm suggestions; formal proposals need a paragraph, while informal need only the last point restated

Letters   To be certain the reader knows what future action will be taken

E-mails   To request an RSVP so your reader knows what to do with your message

A concluding Power 1 sentence or paragraph is NOT important in:

News/Press Releases
Contact information at the start of document regarding person/product/business is sufficient

Public Service Announcements
General facts presented to the public—such as flu shot availability, worth fundraisers, a special children's event—do not need reiteration

Memos   Why repeat what was already stated?

E-mail threads   Let your conscience be your guide

✍ Practice: Write a concluding Power 1 sentence

Use any of the approaches above to add a concluding Power 1 sentence or paragraph to these scenarios. Once again, I've given you an example.

1. The conclusion to your monthly newsletter:

The best move you can make is to talk to one of the professionals I've mentioned here. Working with a financial professional who is knowledgeable about the options available will benefit you in the short and the long run.

The writer wrapped up the article succinctly in two sentences.

2. An e-mail responding to a customer complaint about services on board your airline
3. A response to an interviewee informing her that she did not get the position for which she applied
4. A wrap-up paragraph for a proposal
5. A cover letter to accompany a job application

✍ Now you try it

Add a concluding Power 1 sentence or paragraph to your draft. Also, reread your introduction. Does it still work with your conclusion?

Dr. Julie Tip:
If your document requires stating conclusions and that's difficult for you, here's a trick you might play on yourself. Instead of trying to summarize the conclusions, try just listing the most interesting or important findings. From that list you can synthesize the information.

Let's focus

Take your draft and give it the *litmus test* below. Then focus *only* on the areas that need reworking.

Answer yes or no to these questions:	Yes	No
Does my writing accomplish my purpose?	____	____
Does it say *enough*?	____	____
Is it clear?	____	____
Are my ideas sequenced so that the reader can easily follow them?	____	____
Have I engaged the reader?	____	____
Does the reader know what to do?	____	____

In other words, have you clearly stated what you want from the reader?

If you answered "no" to any of the above questions, use your time and energy to revise your document so that you can answer "yes" to all the questions.

A writer's best friend is the waste-paper basket.
-Isaac Singer

Rewrite Quickly and Painlessly

All good writers rework their words. When Ernest Hemingway was asked by George Plimpton, who was working for the *Paris Review* at the time, about the process of rewriting, the great writer confessed, "I rewrote the ending of *A Farewell to Arms*, the last page of it, thirty-nine times before I was satisfied." Plimpton probed, "Were there some technical problems there? What was it that had stumped you?" Hemingway's reply: "Getting the words right."

Getting the words right

Getting the words right means taking a cold, hard look at your writing, trading the free-wheeling fedora you've worn up to this point for the critic's cap, and calling up those internal writing police to sharpen their red pencils.

Why? Because you need to adopt the attitude that this part of the writing process is the fun part! Does it involve work? Sure—I'd be lying if I said it didn't. But it's in the revising and rewriting that your imaginative problem-solving skills come into play. You get to scratch your head, step back, and think about how you can clearly and effectively communicate your message to your reader. And, with practice, you will gain both speed and skill.

So, a pause before you begin your rewrite...

Or as Tom said pointlessly, "My pencil is dull."

That's just what you want—a dull pencil—so that you will be forced to stop, step back, and get time and distance from your draft before you start sharpening your words. As author E.B. White advised in *The New Yorker* magazine, "Let the body heat go out" of your writing.

> *No passion in the world is equal to the passion to alter someone else's draft.*
> *-H.G. Wells*

On the following pages, you'll take your draft and refine it. You'll work on style by getting the words right so that your message gets read. You'll see how transitions guide the reader through your document. But most noteworthy, you'll find this process relatively quick and painless—*if* you paid attention! So as you continue to rewrite, review:

Dr. Julie's Five Guiding Principles Plus One

1 **Allow an hour or two away from your first draft;** overnight is even better, assuming your boss doesn't want it by the close of business today. You will come back with fresh eyes and ears and really be able to see "where the shoe pinches."

2 **Always read your writing out loud.** You may read with your eyes, but your ears will give you a much better idea of the cadence, the inflection, and the rhythm of your text. You will also discover where your writing makes sense and where a question mark goes off in your head.

3 **Remember the "So what?" factor.** Visualize your readers with those words tattooed on their forehead as you write. So what do they care? So what do they understand? So what should they do with your message?

4 **Set aside time to write,** especially if you are knee-deep in a project. Make an appointment with yourself, preferably at the same time each day. Turn off the phones, the coworkers, or any other distractions. You'll be surprised how much you can get done in thirty minutes, let alone an hour.

5 **Run don't walk to the nearest bookstore or computer screen** and purchase these essential books. These "must-haves" ought to sit at your work station:

- *The Elements of Style*, William Strunk Jr. and E. B. White. The ultimate authorities on style. This concise, straightforward book will cover most of your writing questions. However, if you want a more in-depth stylebook, consider *The Gregg Reference Manual* (my editor's favorite), *The Chicago Manual of Style*, or *The MLA Style Manual and Guide to Scholarly Publishing*.

- *Webster's Collegiate Dictionary (current edition)*. No little wimpy paperback, but a real thick book.

- *Roget's International Thesaurus*. Get the big one with tabs. Do not rely on any software program to give you the depth and breadth of words that this book can deliver.

> Dr. Julie Tip:
> If you're looking for pithy or memorable sayings to add to your document, check out some of the Web sites that list quotes. Search under the phrase *memorable quotes*. They could be used in a sales letter or brochure, even an executive summary or speech.

6 When you write with a group...

If you're called on to create a document with the help of others, Idea Mapping and Power Numbering still work. Here are a few other tips for group writing:

- If you work best thinking through the topic alone before meeting with your group, give yourself a couple of days after all the research is in to absorb and analyze the information. Then you can formulate some conclusions before meeting with your group again.

- Try to limit the group to six people. More than that makes the process too complicated.

- Be sure key players and decision makers are in the loop. Waiting until the document is done is *not* the time to ask for feedback.

- If you have grant writers, public information officers, or a marketing department, bring these experts in for a consult. They have an uncanny ability to quickly get to the point. Who knows, maybe they'll even offer to help write!

Remember Rule-Breaker Number One: Throw Out the Formal Outline? Well, before we continue, I need to give you permission to break another rule:

Rule-Breaker Number Two: Write Like You Talk!

I know your teachers said that writing was a completely different language than speaking, but they were WRONG! Your writing needs to sound like a conversation you would have with your reader.

In the world of business, writing is expected to be professional. But "professional" does not mean a formal, stiff style or manner that makes it difficult for you to connect with your reader. In fact, the trend over the past ten years has been to move away from the formal, academic style to a more conversational, informal one.

Imagine explaining a process, describing a new product, conducting a personnel evaluation, or reviewing the year-end report.

No conscientious writer should complain of the trouble. Writing is a social act: whoever claims his neighbor's attention by writing is duty-bound to take the trouble—and in any case, what is life for, unless to do at least some right things?

—Jacques Barzun

See yourself sitting at your desk, standing in the conference room with your peers, or talking on the phone with a client.

You would speak in a normal, logically sequenced, conversational manner, using the appropriate language and voice for your audience. You would establish rapport, showing who you are.

That's the voice you want to project in your writing. Your writing should sound like conversation, only better, because you wouldn't have "uhs" or "ums" or use slang. Let your personality show through.

Technical writing

Even in technical writing, where you are allowed less latitude in how you present the material, you can define terms, present examples, include anything necessary to make your writing easier to understand. Though the tone stays professional and objective, the writing still needs to be readable. Or don't you care if they read your report?

If you're still not sure about making your writing less formal, consider the presidential decree that requires government agencies to put their words in more user-friendly language. The *Plain Language* initiative insists that agencies write clear, understandable communication. For example, rather than writing:

Grant applications must provide the following information...

They recommend:
When you apply for a grant, you must send us...

Another example—rather than:
nature of in-kind match being provided...

They recommend:
A description of the in-kind match you will provide...

*Not writing in plain English has gotten cities and municipalities in hot water. For example, poorly written intiatives have been misunderstood and citizens erroneously have **voted down** bills that would have increased state funding!*

Which is easier to read? Look at this example from the Plain Language Web site (www.plainlanguage.gov).

Before:

For good reasons, the Secretary may grant extensions of time in 30-day increments for filing of the lease and all required bonds, provided that additional extension requests are submitted and approved before the expiration of the original 30 days or the previously granted extension.

After:

We may extend the time you have to file the lease and required bonds. Each extension will be for a 30-day period. To get an extension, you must write to us giving the reasons you need more time. We must receive your extension request in time to approve it before your current deadline or extension expires.

Simple Guide to Plain Language

It remains your responsibility to get your points across, to define the issues concisely, to help the people who read your writing understand what you are saying. So **write like you speak**: simple, direct sentences, crisp explanations, clear images, ordinary words with a professional but personal touch.

Let's be clear. I'm not talking about chatting up the reader—that's not appropriate. I'm suggesting that you avoid a pedantic (highfalutin', flashy, affected, stilted) style that turns your reader off and wastes time. Take a look at the following *Simple Guide to Plain Language.*

A Simple Guide to Plain Language

Pedantic	Readable
ascertain	find out
aforementioned	these
as a result of	because
at this point in time	now
before long	soon
cease	stop
commence	start, begin
compensate	pay
correspondence	letter
demonstrate	show
desire	want
due to the fact	because
during the time that	while
elect	choose
facilitate	ease/help
for the purpose of	to
give consideration to	consider
implement	do
in close proximity	near
in the future	soon
in the event that	if
indebtedness	debt
indicate	show
in view of the fact that	since
locate	find
numerous	many
on condition that	provided
prior to	before
purchase	buy
rapid	fast
reason is because	reason is
residence	address
subsequent to	after
subsequently	later
sufficient	enough
terminate	end
utilize	use
vehicle	car/tool

I deliberately used the word "pedantic" to make a point! Note that my tongue is firmly planted in my cheek.

Mark Twain makes the point about unnecessary verbosity quite eloquently: "I never write 'metropolis' for seven cents when I can get the same price for 'city.'" Syndicated columnist James J. Kilpatrick asked his readers: "What is the purpose of writing anyhow? ... It seems to me, it is not to enlarge our readers' vocabularies but to communicate an idea from the mind of the writer to the mind of the reader." **So write like you talk.**

What's write? What's wrong?

You judge! Look at these examples of pedantic writing.

An e-mail sent to a design team:

> *Team,*
> *Per an e-mail from Mary last week informing me of the decision to delay the conversion of DXM into RLM, and in order to gain optimum utilization of the by-products of our refining activities, we can simultaneously achieve economic advantage from our selling activities if we utilize the sizing solution.*

Do you even have a clue what this says? An opening description on the home page of a well-known software company's Web site:

> *(Company name) is endeavorily* determined to promote constant attention on current procedures of transacting business focusing emphasis on innovative ways to better, if not supersede, the expectations of quality!*

* Not a word in *my* dictionary

With all due respect, Mr. Greenspan:

Whether incipient bubbles can be detected in real time and whether, once detected, they can be defused without inadvertently precipitating still greater adverse consequences for the economy remain in doubt.

Mr. Alan Greenspan, the former chairman of the Federal Reserve Board *(The New York Times)*

From a manufacturing company to its employees:

Outline the ongoing process to validate and strengthen the Business Continuity Program. The Exercise Program is a high-level description of exercise or test plans which include development, implementation, critique and documentation process. An Exercise Plan is a detailed collection of objectives, tasks, roles and responsibilities to guide the exercise participants through a single exercise.

Have I made my point?!

Dr. Julie Tip:

If you find it difficult to write like you talk, try these ideas:

- Imagine a friend sitting across from you. Start talking about your topic.
- Talk into a tape recorder.
- Call a friend and actually talk through your topic; then write it down just as you said it.
- Use simple words and short sentences.
- Use contractions—but be careful! Contractions denote a more informal writing style.
- Use personal pronouns like: I, me, my, our, you, your, we, us.

! *If you want to see the ultimate example of pretentious and pedantic writing, check out William Lutz's Doublespeak.*

Practice: Rewrite

Rewrite these pedantic, verbose phrases (Answers in the Appendix.)

Pedantic	Rewritten
1. Please be advised that...	Please consider...
2. Reference is made to your letter...	
3. Pursuant to your instructions...	
4. The question as to whether...	
5. Answer in the affirmative. . .	
6. For the reason that. . .	
7. In the near future. . .	

Now you try it

Go to your draft. Eliminate or revise any language that won't connect *you* with the reader.

Adding Transitions

Let's continue to refine your writing by adding words that link ideas and make it easy for the reader to follow your line of thinking.

A **transition** is a word, a phrase, or a sentence that helps the reader to see how your ideas connect. Transition words guide (or signal) your reader. They link your ideas together.

Transition words move the topic forward. They smooth out style, tell the reader what's coming next, or remind the reader what occurred.

French writer Anatole France said that writing is like carpentry and like carpentry "...you must join your sentences smoothly."

Words like the following are commonly used to help the reader:

first	second	however	next
finally	therefore	another	in addition
besides	for example	moreover	furthermore

Always use the simplest transition devices you can, and never overuse them. Otherwise, your writing will sound stilted, stylized, or patronizing. The example below of transition overkill shows how overuse can insult or irritate the reader.

People have always wanted to fly. *However,* until 1903 it remained merely a dream. *For example,* it was believed that human beings should not fly. *Specifically,* they were not birds. *Nevertheless,* the Wright brothers launched the world's first flying machine. *Consequently,* flying today in an airplane is part of our daily lives.

! *If the writer had eliminated even two of the above transitions, the reader would have been a much happier camper.
Just read it aloud and you'll see! Also, poor use of transitions
creates boring sentence structure. Note that every sentence above
is subject-verb.*

Here's an example that works:

> *Where's the economy headed, anyway?* First *it was the
> Goldilocks economy—not too hot and not too cold.* Then
> *the bears came home and Goldilocks was in trouble.* Now
> *it seems Goldilocks is settling down to a nice bowl of
> bear stew.*
>
> The Seattle Times

And another one:

> *The* first *one contends that the terrorist attacks have trans-
> formed everything. The* second *theory holds that Sept. 11
> and the war against terrorism will bring old divides into
> sharper focus.*
>
> Los Angeles Times

✍ Now you try it

Add transitions to your draft. (But don't overdo it!)
Refer to the list of transition words in the Appendix and try
some out. Get a sense of which ones work or sound appropriate. You'll know.

Tricky transitions

Another method of transitioning between ideas consists of using what I call "tricky transitions." In the hands
of a skilled writer, they prove very effective.

Tricky transitions can be used three different ways:

1 **Repetition of a word or phrase from one sentence to the next.** Examples of repetition of a word or phrase:

From the moment [John] Stanford arrived in September, it was clear he'd never be a caretaker or a status-quo manager. **He was** *a change agent...***He was** *the two-star Army general who talked unabashedly about loving children.*

The Seattle Times

2 **Reference to an idea or a phrase from the previous sentence or paragraph.** An example of bringing an idea along:

Two other e-mail improvements are most welcome: First is the addition of **signatures** *that can be tacked on to the end of every e-mail note and give a particular flair to one's electronic correspondence. These* **signatures** *can be utilitarian, such as one's name, address, phone number, etc. They also can be a* **favorite saying.**

The word *signatures* is repeated in the second and fourth sentence. The third sentence uses *they* to refer to the topic of the paragraph: e-mail signatures.

Among my **favorite** *signatures from notes I have received have been, "Bigamy: having too many husbands; Monogamy: having too many husbands."*

The Seattle Times

Just for fun: Figure out the Power Numbers to the sentences above. (Answer in Appendix).

3 **Use of pronouns (he, she, it, etc.). The pronouns refer to ideas or people previously mentioned.**

He *didn't get it last summer when the trouble began.* **He** *didn't get it last month when the problems multiplied. And,* **he** *still doesn't get it.*

The Wall Street Journal

In this memo, Mr. Brown repeats the phrase *renaming the streets* as his transitional device. It certainly drives the point home to the reader.

And just for fun see if you can determine the Power Numbers sentence structure of this memo. (Answer in Appendix)

Memo
To: *City Council members*
From: *Jason Brown, President, Chamber of Commerce*
Re: *Renaming streets*
Date: *February 18, XXXX*

I was surprised to read in the Woodway Weekly *about the city council's decision to change the street names as it creates considerable hardship for the entire business community. First,* **renaming the streets** *could cause a loss of revenue for business owners. New street names will only confuse customers trying to locate us. Second,* **renaming the streets** *forces us to spend unnecessarily. All our marketing materials—from stationery to cards to billing to brochures—will have to be redone. I find this totally unacceptable! Last,* **renaming the streets** *appears to be change for change's sake. Since the founding of this city, we have always had numbered streets. What's the hidden agenda here?*

Now you try it

Go through your draft and see where you could add a tricky transition. Once you've done that, check your draft. Do you have:

- ❑ A Power Number structure that is appropriate for the audience?
- ❑ A document that is reader-friendly?
- ❑ An appropriate tone for your audience?
- ❑ A document that accomplishes what you want?
- ❑ Enough information to address your readers' questions and concerns?

Now review your entire document and consider the following questions as well:

A Writer's Checklist

√ Does the Power 1 state the purpose of your document?

√ Does your introduction capture your readers' attention?

√ Do your Power 2s (sentences or paragraphs) discuss your Power 1?

√ Do you provide enough examples and supporting points (Power 3s) to be clear?

√ Does the paper have a logical organization?

√ Do you maintain focus on your topic?

√ Did you provide enough transitions to help guide your reader?

√ Does your conclusion restate the intent of the document without repeating the exact wording?

√ Do your introduction and conclusion work well together?

In Summary

Rewriting is what good writing is all about. Take heart! Look at what these two writing experts said half-jokingly about the process of rewriting:

A clear sentence is no accident. Very few sentences come out right the first time, or even the third time. Remember, this is a consolation in moments of despair.

William Zinsser

A lot depends on having the right spirit: businesslike and detached. A certain ruthlessness is best of all. Not desperate-ruthlessness, "Oh God, this is awful. I've got to change everything," but breezy-ruthlessness, "Yes, this certainly does have some problems."

Peter Elbow

What's Next

In the next chapter, you will:
- Review the C.L.E.V.R. solutions to business writing.
- Drill deeper to further streamline your writing.
- Understand the importance of clear and concise writing.
- Learn what to avoid and what to eliminate.
- Know how to use feedback *correctly.*
- Practice adding a variety of sentence patterns.
- Use the six economical tips.
- Break some rules and follow others.

Are we having fun yet?

CHAPTER FOUR

GET SMART

C.L.E.V.R. Solutions to Business Writing

I have good news and more good news! First: Merely reading your writing aloud can eliminate 60 percent of all your writing errors. That leaves only 40 percent with which you need concern yourself. Second: Out of that remaining 40 percent, you probably only have a few writing issues that you need to work on. And third: *Practice makes permanent.* If, as you review each of the C.L.E.V.R. solutions, you spend time practicing them, they will then become a permanent part of your writing repertoire.

Practice makes permanent!

And no, C.L.E.V.R. is not a spelling error. It's a mnemonic device for helping you remember the solutions to your professional writing concerns. Mnemonic, a technique for improving memory, associates familiar words with new or unfamiliar words or concepts. Therefore, C.L.E.V.R. will help you remember the methods to use as you face your writing tasks. *A thought*: Use these solutions along with a good dose of common sense.

In the last chapter, you worked at developing a logical flow to your writing. Here you will drill deeper and review how to refine your words. So, let's begin.

! *Remember: Everything in moderation. Your goal is productivity, not perfectionism.*

"C" Stands for Clarity

Clarity in writing results from good organization of your ideas. *Pat yourself on the back! Take a bow!* You've already accomplished *that* by using the Power Numbers system. Expressing exactly what you mean is the essence of clear writing and clear thinking. Always strive to make your writing as direct, orderly, and precise as possible.

Don't write merely to be understood. Write so you cannot possibly be misunderstood.
-Robert Louis Stevenson

Clarity means: Simplify your writing

The pressure of time does not excuse unclear or confusing writing. Poor writing could cost your business time, money, energy, prestige, and even a lawsuit!

Simple is best, yet tough to do. These ponderously written examples desperately need repair.

Practice: Rewrite for clarity

Turn these muddied sentences into simple, clear prose. See one possible way to rewrite these sentences in the Appendix.

I've done the first one for you:

1. A significant amount of the inventory appears to be improperly positioned in order to meet instantaneous shipping conditions. Furthermore, some portion of the quarterly lost sales was directly generated by the inability to effectively and efficiently transport our inventory.

Rewritten: *Seventy-five percent of quarterly sales were lost by the inability to quickly move inventory. Therefore, we need to reposition it to meet shipping requests.*

2. We are enthusiastic about the opportunity to serve you and work with your people in this extremely important undertaking. We have the utmost confidence in our ability to help you to achieve a profitable organization through the repositioning of your market.

3. If you desire to have a modification as requested, you must apply to the appropriate department for this exemption. The deregulation policy requirement manual is attached and must be signed, dated, and returned. You should also plan to write this office as you were instructed in the letter of May XXXX.

> *Get your facts first, then you can distort them as much as you please!*
> *-Mark Twain*

4. Due to the unexpected and continued high demand of our users covered under the Platinum Plan, it will now be necessary to change the rates by adjusting them effective July XXXX.

Some pretty clear stories

These tales from the front line help make my point.

A telecommunication consultant stated that government RFPs must have clear language or they won't be granted. "Unless the reviewers can understand our specs, all our hard work gets tossed in the circular file!"

A CEO of a large urban hospital says that clarity in communication is what he seeks in his writing. "I have to write responses to projects and programs undertaken in other areas of the country or other institutions. These documents require clarity of thought. The opposite has reflected negatively on me and my institution and destroyed our chances for funding."

A hazardous waste company got an unexpected surprise when the proposal they submitted to a longstanding client was rejected. They considered this a "no-brainer" contract, so they put out little effort and simply cut and pasted old verbiage. To their surprise, they lost out to the competition. Why? The words did not convey clearly and concisely that they could really do the job.

Clarity means: Eliminate the ultimate weasel word: *There*

As you work to make your writing clearer, more concise, and more dynamic, eliminate the word *there* in your sentences. The word is useful for referring to a place, but starting a sentence with *there* does not produce engaging prose and should be expunged forever from your writing. A strong statement? No! *There*, virtually a non-word, can't really be diagrammed (wouldn't Sister be proud) and can force you into using *to be* verbs.

Starting sentences *there is, there was, there has been, there will be*, and so on is simply a lazy way of writing. By removing this "weasel word," you will deliver your message more clearly and keep the reader interested.

Review the following examples and see how much brighter the sentences are without "there."

- There are five indispensable time management habits.

Your passbook to a full and rich life lies in practicing five indispensable time management habits.

- There is a difference between the stated policy and actual practice in this organization.

The stated policy and actual practice differ in this organization.

- There are four money-saving ideas with our new customer service plan.
Our new customer service plan offers four money-saving ideas.

- There are several alternatives to this reorganization design.
Several alternatives to this reorganization design deserve consideration.

Practice: Eliminate *there*

Rewrite these sentences, eliminating *there* at the beginning. See one possible way to rewrite these sentences in the Appendix.

1. There are scads of scanners on the market, some really inexpensive. (*The Wall Street Journal*)
2. There are legal ramifications that go along with each 911 call.
3. There are three good stock buys in the technology sector.
4. There has been a lot of grant writing done in this department.
5. There is a clear definition for "medical eligibility."
6. There's a lot that's cool about digital photography. (*The Wall Street Journal*)
7. There will be lots more before the dust settles. (*The Seattle Times*)

Now you try it

You didn't put that draft away did you? Get it out and see if any of your sentences contain the dreaded "there."

Clarity means: Saying "No!" to the verb "to be"

Beware of *to be* verbs such as *is, am, are, was, were, be, been, being.* Whenever you can, use more interesting, more specific, and more varied verbs than the ubiquitous old standby *to be*. Where you can purge them from your sentences for these four reasons:

1 They often introduce passive voice.
Simply speaking, passive voice means that whoever performed the action gets second-class citizenship. For example, the sentence *The baseball was hit by Babe Ruth* is passive. Ruth did the hitting and he doesn't even get top billing! The baseball gets all the glory. To make the sentence active, you would write *Babe Ruth hit the baseball.* (And probably over the fence.)

Think of passive voice as the opposite of active (as in "action") voice. In active voice the subject of the sentence performs the action, while in the passive voice, the subject is acted upon.

For example the sentence *The road was repaired by the construction crew* uses the passive voice. The people who actually did the work appear at the end of the sentence. Look what happens to the crew in the active voice: *The construction crew repaired the road.* In this sentence whoever performed the action remains upfront.

2 You get more bang for your buck and in fewer words.
Eliminating unnecessary *to be* verbs often gives the reader more information with fewer words. By rewriting the sentences (in #1) above they became 20 percent shorter, more vigorous, and much easier to understand! Count the difference in these two examples:

The letter was received by the manager. (passive)
versus
The manager received the letter. (active)

The second sentence becomes shorter, more direct with active voice.

The meeting was held by our department. (passive)
versus
Our department held a meeting. (active)

With active voice, you know right away who performed the action.

*Please be advised that your concern will be addressed and
you will be contacted when the difficulty is determined.*
(passive)

versus

We will contact you once we discover the problem. (active)

3 *To be* **verbs do your reader no favors.**
Eliminating as many of these verbs as possible
will go a long way to mak-
ing your writing more
exciting and less wordy.
When you write without
using the *to be* verb as a convenient crutch, you force
yourself to become more creative. The following example
illustrates this point.

*The active voice strikes
like a boxer moving
forward in attack; the
passive voice parries
while back-pedaling.*
    -Theodore Bernstein

*There was a lively discussion among our team on Monday. We
are 100 percent happy about the new product ideas and are in
agreement about the benefits to the customer. We believe that
customers will be happy about the changes and will be willing
to respond with enthusiasm and money.*

Now look at it rewritten with a minimum of *to be* verbs
(and where used, they provide impact).

*After a lively discussion on Monday, we whole-heartedly
endorsed the new product ideas. We all agreed that customers
would clearly see the benefits, embrace the changes, and
respond with enthusiasm and money.*

4 *To be* **verbs can cause confusion.**
Look at this example from *Gregg Reference Manual*:

*A computer was reported stolen over the weekend by the
security guard.*

I smell a lawsuit! The passive voice in this sentence unintentionally points a finger at the wrong doer.

Here it is rewritten: *The head of corporate security reported the theft of two computers over the weekend.*

By getting rid of as many *to be* verbs as possible you will accomplish two things:

• Your sentences virtually leap off the page with fresh, dynamic language.

• Your sentences become clear and concise.

✐ Practice: Eliminate *to be*

Eliminate the *to be (is, am, are, was, were, be, been, being)* verbs in the following sentences. See one possible way to rewrite these sentences in the Appendix.

1. The situation was studied by the committee.
2. Insurance is sold by this company.
3. Evaluation tools are used by our managers to keep our programs running smoothly.
4. Good writing is hard work.*
5. It was noted that it is believed that proposal "C" would be less expensive.

An important bird walk. Sometimes by simply changing the position of the words in the sentence, you can eliminate the *to be* verb. Other times, you will have to work a little harder. You probably found the first three sentences above fairly easy to change and the fourth a little more difficult. It could be rewritten: **Good writing involves/consists of/requires hard work.*

✐ Now you try it

Take out a highlighter and give your draft to a trusted peer. Have him/her circle those *to be* verbs. Then rewrite those sentences. You now get a break and can let your draft rest. Try your hand at some of the practices coming up.

Is all passive voice wrong?

I hope I have made the case for active voice, which in most instances remains the best choice. But is all passive voice usage wrong? Of course not! The key word in that sentence? *Usage.* You don't want to go through verbal gyrations just to avoid all passive verbs, because the outcome may end up stilted or phony. The use of passive voice can work in the following situations:

1 **In technical and scientific reports, the result often represents the most important piece of information given within a sentence.** By using passive voice, the result becomes the subject and you help maintain objectivity. For example:

The volume of the fluid was decreased by 5 percent by adding sodium.

A new species of butterfly was discovered on the latest expedition to Central America.

The importance here is *what* was done not *who* did it.

2 **Sensitive situations that require tact and diplomacy may dictate the use of passive voice.** To avoid pointing fingers at the doer of the action in the following examples, which would you write?

Your sales team did not meet the quarterly profit goals.
or
The profit goals were not met this quarter.

The engineers designed defective plane parts.
or
The plane parts were not designed correctly.

3 In some instances the writer may not be able to identify who did the action, the action has more interest than the actor, or *no* doer is needed to make the sentence work:

All the computer files were erased.

Mr. Brown was killed at a construction site.

Governor Smith was hit by a car.

Although you want to use active voice whenever possible, passive voice will creep into your writing. Just use it as you would expensive perfume—sparingly, provocatively, and in the right spots.

Remember, common sense and moderation prevail. You do not have to completely eliminate *to be* verbs from your writing, just temper their use. Could Shakespeare have written Hamlet's immortal lines—*To be or not to be: that is the question*—any other way and with such impact?

A word is not a crystal: transparent and unchanged; it is the skin of a living thought and may vary greatly in color and content according to the circumstances and time in which it is used.

–Oliver Wendell Holmes

Two more *clear* thoughts

By writing concisely and precisely, you will gain clarity. Choosing just the right words makes your intent clear to your reader. That means crisp sentences with precise words *and* no excess. Notice the difference between these pairs of words:

profitable, productive
lucrative, well-paying
lost, forfeited
divested, ruined

Each has a slightly different definition. Precision in word choice aids your reader. So get out that dictionary and thesaurus!

Writing clearly and effectively also means putting in specifics—time, place, numbers, or names—where appropriate. It makes you just that much more credible.

Which is clearer and more precise?

Recently we have seen a gradual increase in profits.

or

Recently we have seen a 20 percent increase in profits.

Expressing exactly what you mean is the essence of clear writing and clear thinking. Yes, it's not always easy to do. To write simply and clearly takes some brainwork, but your reader deserves the effort.

"L" Stands for Language

I've mentioned the importance of writing for your reader: keeping your tone, your voice, your words, the language in the document tailored to the specific audience. Now I present what to avoid and—what to use in your writing.

Avoid clichés

Try to avoid clichés as much as possible. Cliches fill business writing because of their obvious familiarity to the writer and the reader. However, expressions like *water off a duck's back, the bottom line, few and far between,* and *which we would do well to bear in mind* can add length and make your writing vague, stale and uninspiring.

Last but not least, bite the bullet and *take the ball and run with it* while reviewing the following.

Tired clichés	Rewritten examples
last but not least	last, finally
venture a guess	estimate
in one fell swoop	suddenly
few and far between	few
the modern business world	business today

Avoid jargon and acronyms

Jargon and acronyms are technical slang (enterprise transformation initiatives) and abbreviations (NIMBY: Not In My Back Yard) unique to a particular occupation or group. They can be just fine and actually save time with in-house communication or when working with those in the same field. In fact, if the dictionary lists the acronym as a word, feel free to use it.

But remember, your audience determines your word choice. Jargon and acronyms that may be very clear in an e-mail sent to your peers, wouldn't be used with the board of directors.

Dr. Julie Tip:
Technology writer Paul Andrews of *The Seattle Times* offers this suggestion: "If you're tired of decoding acronyms go to http:www.acronymfinder.com. Type in the acronym and the site searches through 70,000 acronyms and returns what it finds."

And if your document goes out to those not in your field, confusion can set in. Consider these supposedly commonplace acronyms:

- CIA also stands for the Culinary Institute of America
- FBI is the acronym of a food and beverage organization
- NATO refers to a theatre owners' organization.
- COLA is governmentese for "cost of living adjustment"

Avoid biased language

Avoid sexist language. Period. I don't need to go into much detail about this subject. Your purpose remains to inform, persuade, or sell—not offend. The list below offers some commonly used sexist terms with alternate suggestions:

Avoid	Use
anchorman	anchor
chairman	chair, chairperson, head
cleaning woman	domestic, housekeeper
draftsman	drafter
fireman	firefighter
foreman	supervisor
housewife	homemaker
mailman	mail carrier
mankind	humankind, humanity
newsman	reporter, journalist
policeman	police officer
salesman	salesperson
spokesman	spokesperson
stewardess	flight attendant
weatherman	weathercaster
workman	worker

Always find out how people prefer to be addressed. Dr.? Ms.? Miss? Mrs.? Professor? Dean? Call and ask. If that's not possible, use Mr. or Ms.

Use descriptive writing

Yes, even in nonfiction writing, a turn of a phrase, a well-placed word can make the difference in the reader's receptivity to your message. Again, organization and clarity rule as you describe a process, a product, or a new service. But you also need to choose and use words that get the reader close to your writing. Using vivid language creates certain images depending on your audience. For instance, you would certainly choose different words for NRA members than you might for the Bartenders Association. First, picture your reader. Then try to choose just the right words that will help your reader understand your message. The following suggestions can help.

Use nouns

Using concrete nouns (*Cadillac, book, piano*) that appeal to one of the five senses is a good technique. Choosing more tangible words helps the reader see, touch, feel, smell, or hear your idea. In contrast, abstract nouns—those that name something intangible such as *religion, poverty, love, courage*—do not provide the reader with a clear image. Look at these sentences below. Which would help the reader get closer to the topic?

> *A product leaked on the floor.*
> versus
> *Gasoline leaked on the shop floor.*

> *We store data.*
> versus
> *We neatly store those mounds of information piled in folders around your desk.*

Here are some descriptive noun examples from print: *A* New York Times *writer helped readers understand what the Mars rover,* Sojourner, *looked like by describing it as about the size of a microwave oven. And Walter Goodman, also from* The New York Times, *wrote about Pat Buchanan: His voice easily beats the enhanced decibel levels of the commercials.*

Use nouns that paint pictures for your readers. Avoid abstract ones that they can't wrap their brain around. Words such as *sadness, gun running,* or *a billion dollars* conjure up more imagery than *emotion, crime,* or *wealth.* How will your descriptions help your reader?

Use similes, metaphors, analogies

Similes, metaphors, and analogies also work. These three figures of speech help the reader understand by comparing two unlike things. Similes are the most concrete of the three. With similes, the words *like* or *as* signal to the reader comparison while metaphors and analogies are subtler in their approach. These techniques help illuminate difficult ideas.

Similes

The following two clever simile examples come from James J. Kilpatrick's weekly column, "The Writer's Art":

From Chicago sportswriter Bob Verdi: *Trying to get a knee-high fastball past Smith is like trying to get a sunrise past a rooster.*

Professor Stephen Hawking, the theoretical physicist, continues to garner recognition, according to Susan Page of *USA Today.* "Hawking's popular appeal seems to come from his...informal language and concrete metaphors.... He makes reasonably understandable such difficult and fundamental questions as the relationship of time and space."

An Arizona Republic *reporter wrote: Suspects are as thick as ticks in timber.*

Two more excellent examples:
From The San Diego Union Tribune, *a sportswriter described the city's annual Crew Classic: As the shell crossed the finish line, the rowers collapsed like marionettes whose strings had been cut.*

Here a real estate tycoon is described in Pacific Magazine: *Bank accounts, stocks and bonds struck him as flimsy as sheets on a clothesline.*

Metaphors

Like similes, metaphors can make your writing that much more inviting and energetic. This example of a metaphor describes what a hotel did when its star chef announced he was leaving:
It turns its search machine on sizzle and sets out to find a replacement faster than a chocoholic can sniff out a double-decadence cheesecake.
                                                    -The Seattle Times

An example from *The New York Times*:
Hillary Rodham Clinton has fewer local roots than a giant cactus.

And from *The Washington Post*:
A reporter discussed a congresswoman "with the voting record more middle of the road than a yellow line."

Just for fun

Caution! These mixed-up metaphors from Richard Lederer's book, *Anguished English*, humorously exemplify how metaphors can go awry:

- The slowdown is accelerating.
- When we get to that bridge, we'll jump.
- It's time to grab the bull by the tail and look it in the eye.
- I do hope that you don't think I've been making a mountain out of a mole hole, but that's the whole kettle of fish in a nutshell.
- Lou Brock, the great St. Louis Cardinal baseball player: *I always felt I was a guy who had the ability to light the spark of enthusiasm which unlocked the hidden geysers of adrenaline that causes one to play to the summit of his ability.*

Analogies

Analogies also serve as an excellent device when you are attempting to explain something unknown to the reader. Particularly useful to technical writers, they help explain information to a nontechnical audience. Look at this example from the *Handbook of Technical Writing:*

The search technique used in this kind of file processing is similar to the search technique use to look up a word in the dictionary.

And again from James Kilpatrick's column, music critic Rita Landrum wrote:

Although Watkins never seemed stiff, he did seem careful throughout the first half, as if he were driving a borrowed Lamborghini. He took it through its paces with great confidence and gave us a thrilling ride, but he didn't seem to own the car until after intermission.

Now you try it

Think about one of your products or services that you have previously described in PR material, and see if you can rework it using strong, concrete nouns. Or practice writing a simile, metaphor, or analogy. Remember, take a familiar topic and add something dissimilar.

"E" Stands for Economy

Economy of writing means you don't waste the reader's time. Being brief but informative will always make you a winner. However, you do not want your writing to be so brief that it shows a lack of thought; your reader still needs details. Rid your writing of rambling sentences, asides, any repetition of ideas for which you have already made your point. Try to shorten your words and your sentences. **Economize** by packing the most meaning into the fewest words. Use these tips below to get to the point!

Whenever you can shorten a sentence, do. The best sentence? The shortest.

-Gustave Flaubert

"Don't dance with me!"

The owner of a large temporary placement service for the technology industry said that when he reads cover letters from applicants, the first words out of his mouth are often "Don't dance with me. Get to the point! I'm busy, overwhelmed with the paper glut, and I don't have time to sift through your sentences to find out if your experience matches with my client's needs. Skip the frills, just give me the facts." (Thank you, Sergeant Friday!)

Dr. Julie Tip:
Be careful that, as you make your points, you pick a few to focus on and go into depth. Unless you're writing a dissertation, depth is more important than breadth in writing.

Six economical tips

1 **Keep sentence length around twenty words.** Reader comprehension drops after that number. Here's where reading your document aloud can help. If you're breathless by the end of a sentence, it's too long. Or count the number of words. Also, sentences can be one word. Honestly.

2 **One- and two-syllable words are best.** Again, the goal remains to express ideas, not impress the reader with your vocabulary. Shorten words where appropriate.

Which of these are easier to see or hear?

Compare these words	To these
countenance	face
publication	book
utilize	use
perambulate	walk
domicile	home

3 **Avoid excessive use of *ion* or *ness*.** Dropping these endings makes for stronger images in your sentences and sometimes turns flat nouns into lively verbs or adjectives.

Rather than	Use
consideration	consider
conclusion	conclude
modification	modify
abbreviation	abbreviate
carefulness	careful
pompousness	pompous
indebtedness	indebted
greediness	greedy

4 **Keep your paragraphs brief with only one idea per paragraph.** When appropriate, paragraphs can even be only one sentence long. Breaks between the paragraphs allow your reader a moment to consider your point. They also give your readers' eyes a break by providing white space on the page.

5 **Use adverbs and adjectives frugally.** You need to lean on strong nouns and verbs as the framework for your sentences. However, often by adding adverbs or adjectives you create more accurate or complete images in the reader's mind. For example, phrases like *clear writing, confusing directions, haphazard growth, misspelled words* use describing words that clarify.

Be careful, though, because when overused or used improperly, adverbs and adjectives detract. Some examples are *most unique, definitely overcrowded, rather cloudy, less superb, supremely tragic.* Those modifiers merely take away.

6 **Eliminate redundancy wherever you can.** Redundancy—the unnecessary repetition of words or concepts—appears so often in our writing that it may go unnoticed. Look carefully for redundancy and excise it from your writing. Some examples of frequently used redundancies follow.

Huh? So the question to be debated on both sides is: Should we refer back to the advance warnings, or postpone until later any further necessary requirements?

Redundant Phrases

absolutely perfect	large (or small) in size
add up	my personal opinion
advance warning	past history
another additional	rectangular in shape
any and all	reduce down
cancel out	return back
combined together	the absolute truth
erase out	the month of May
fall down	yellow in color
hurry up	8 a.m. in the morning

! *In technical writing, the need for accuracy can make the reiteration of key points helpful to the reader. And you saw in Chapter Three how the repetition of phrases, in the right context, can be very effective. Just remember to use moderation. Don't cripple the impact of your words by crowding too many together. Words have power and create images; use too many and your reader won't get your message.*

Practice: Rewrite redundant phrases

See one possible way to rewrite these phases in the appendix.

Rewrite the following phrases:
1. final conclusion
2. 4:00 PM in the afternoon
3. perplexing problems
4. cooperatively working together
5. immediately without delay
6. prearranged strategy
7. commute back and forth

What's write and what's wrong?

From what you have learned thus far, how would you write this letter below? How would you respond if this were sent to you? Wouldn't you love *the opportunity* to strangle Dr. QRX?

Dear Ms. Hollinger:

I am writing this letter to notify my patients that I will be transferring from ABC Medical Center to XYZ Medical Center. I do this with mixed feelings because I have enjoyed the opportunity to participate in your health care, but the opportunity presented itself for me to cut back on my time commitments, affording me the opportunity to spend more time with my family.

I have the opportunity to share a practice with Dr. Doe and I look forward to this opportunity.

I would like to take this opportunity to thank you for the opportunity to participate in your health care.

Best wishes,
Dr. QRX

Dr. Julie Tip:
Always print out your draft. It is easier to review your writing off a hard copy than on the computer screen. Something about seeing the whole of it helps. Double-spacing the draft for ease of reading and revising is also a good idea. And make changes using a pen with colored ink so that your edits will be easy to pick up.

"V" Stands for Variety

I've recommended you read your writing aloud so you can hear what it really sounds like. Your ear remains the best guide for determining whether you are maintaining a conversation with the reader. As you speak, your sentences have variety naturally. They ebb and flow, sometimes start with verbs, ask questions, etc. So, too, must your writing mirror that expressive variety.

Varying the construction of your sentences, the word order, as well as the length, is important; otherwise, you might put your reader to sleep! Variety means:

- Don't anesthetize the reader.
- Construct your sentences differently.
- Vary your writing style with sentence patterns.
- Creatively place punctuation as a way to add interest.

Vary the structure

Did you know that sentences can be constructed in thirty-nine different ways or patterns? That means you have no excuse for falling into the old subject-verb-object trap. By varying the pattern of your sentences, you keep your readers alert. You don't want your writing sounding like the messages on an ATM.

The following example, though extreme, makes the case:

You can't have every sentence sound the same. You would bore your reader to death. You would not sustain the interest of the recipient. Your monotonous words would put your reader's brain in a coma. Your writing would lack interest and variety.

Are you still awake?

Let's take a look at some examples of how a traditional sentence might be rewritten to give it more interest and power.

Here is the comfortable, standard style: *The third-quarter profits exceeded expectations.*

- You could ask a question:
  How much did the third-quarter profits exceed expectations?

- You could use a quotation:
  The chairman of the board gleefully announced, "The third-quarter profits exceeded my expectations!"

- You could begin with a preposition:
  During this third quarter, profits exceeded expectations.

- You could begin with an adverb:
  Giddily, the chairman described the third-quarter profits.

- You could begin with a gerund or -ing verb:
  Praising his sales force, the chairman stated that third-quarter profits exceeded all expectations.

- You could use an appositive:
  Mr. Ross, chairman of the board, announced the third-quarter profits.

- You could use a present infinitive:
  To announce the third-quarter profits, Mr. Ross held a special meeting.

- You could start with an adjective:
  Ecstatic, Mr. Ross announced the third-quarter profits.

- You could write a compound sentence:
  Mr. Ross was pleased with the profits, but he expressed concern about the continued health of the company.

- You could use a parenthetical expression between the subject and the verb:
  The third-quarter profits, in contrast with last quarter, will boost the company's bottom line.

In other words, vary your sentences. See how many different ways you can express that idea!

One strategy that professional writers use to create interest and variety is to place three or four long sentences together followed by a short sentence. This technique can make your writing seem more like a conversation. Or, you can reverse this process by placing a few short sentences before a long one as in this example from a phone company mailer:

> *Sounds great, doesn't it? Well, it gets even better. You can sign up for Call Forwarding from BellCo now and get one month FREE.*

Parallel is powerful

Parallel structure also adds variety. Writers use parallel structure when they list items within a sentence or a paragraph or down a page. For example, discussion points for the next meeting, attributes of a new product, instructions to a client, or questions for an interviewee could be listed in phrases, or sentences, or with bullets, or with numbers. Each phrase/sentence in the list must start the same way. If the first item on the list starts with a verb, all items on the list must start with

What is written without effort is, in general, read without pleasure.
-Samuel Johnson

verbs. If your list (below) starts with a noun, all items must start with nouns. If your list begins with a complete sentences, all items must be in complete sentence. (We'll talk more about listing in Chapter Five.) In this example, the bulleted items started with an adjective:

We will work with you to determine what system best meets your needs, whether your goal is:

- *Improved customer relationships*
- *Reduced inventory costs*
- *Targeted one-on-one marketing*
- *Strategic business planning*
- *Quicker customer notifications*

Parallel structure can also be used within a sentence. Again, the words or phrases must be the same. For example:

The bank offers savings, checking, lending, and trust services.

And coming back to Mr. Ross, the CEO from page 112, we see a good example of parallel structure:

At the board meeting, Mr. Ross announced the profits for the third quarter, the names of the division supervisors, and the beginning date for the new product roll-out.

Dr. Julie Tip:
This technique also works well when you are writing a résumé. List your accomplishments using parallel construction.

Combine your sentences

Another way to add variety to your writing is through sentence combining. Take two sentences that relate to each other and condense them into one. See how it works with these examples:

Listen to what happens when you take these sentences:

Mr. Ross called a meeting. He was laughing. He announced the third-quarter profits.

...and combined them to read:

At the meeting, Mr. Ross laughed as he announced the third-quarter profits.

Let's look at a Power 2 paragraph from Chapter Two on time management.

Before:
Fourth, setting short- and long-range goals should be an ingrained habit. The process consists of deciding what levels of importance each of them have. Then you organize your tasks around achieving them.

Words are all we have.
-Samuel Beckett

After:
The last two sentences have been changed and combined:

The process consists of deciding the levels of importance of each and organizing the tasks around achieving them.

Now you try it

Go back to your draft and look at your Power 2 and Power 3 sentences. Can they be combined without creating a sentence that is too long? Look at your Zero Power sentence. Could it be revised to flow into your Power 1 sentence? Make changes that add fluency and variety to your writing.

Punctuation adds punch

Chapter Five discusses punctuation in detail. At this point, you just need to know that punctuation can speak for you. Since you are not speaking to your reader face to face, punctuation marks can take the place of gestures, voice inflection, and facial expressions.

Dashes —
exclamation points !
question marks ?
colons :
semi-colons ;
and commas ,
...all add variety and interest to your writing. They also provide signposts that guide your reader.

"R" Stands for Rules

Some rules can be broken; others cannot. I've talked about breaking rules that get in the way of getting organized (Chapter One) and getting started (Chapter Two). Below are rules you may want to follow:

A pessimist is a man who looks both ways before crossing a oneway street.
-Lawrence Peter

1 **Use a positive tone.** How your attitude towards a subject comes across to the reader is called *tone.* Are you funny, terse, serious, formal, casual, patronizing, enthusiastic, positive? Knowing your reader is half the battle; the other half is avoiding words that may be negative.

Consider the opening sentence of this letter:

Dear Ms. Bennett:

We regret to learn about your bad experience with our plant manager.

Now see what happens when you take out the negative words, state the facts as you see them, and change the tone to reflect a positive point of view.

Dear Ms. Bennett:

Thank you for informing us about the quality of service you received last week. Our plant manager has asked that I send you his apologies. I have also enclosed the following information about your recent order.

Words such as *never, no, not, won't, can't, failed* and other negatives need to be replaced with more positive words.

Some negative words to avoid		
failure	sorry	blame
problem	complaint	impossible
intolerable	neglect	negligence
waste	weak	wrong
worry	careless	change
mistake	biased	exaggerate
abandon	cheap	evade
low	senseless	vague
useless	deny	ruin
misfortune	misguided	discredit
dispute	unfortunate	pointless
inefficient	abrupt	unfair

 Positively mind your manners. Always remember *please* and *thank you*. Be courteous without gushing. More about e-tiquette (electronic etiquette) in Chapter Six.

Be personable. Keep *you* in your writing. Remember, if you depersonalize your writing too much, you won't make a connection with the reader.

Before:

Department heads are hereby requested to comply with facility utilization procedures by forwarding the required documentation twenty-four hours prior to usage.

After:
To avoid double booking conference rooms, please send your request twenty-four hours in advance.

That's why using *you, he, she,* and *I* help build the rapport that words like *people, one,* and *individual* do not. Also, adding personal experiences creates interest. If that seems difficult for you, use quoted remarks from others.

Other ways to be personable:

- Let the reader know what you can do for him/her.

- If appropriate, use the reader's name in the body of the document.

- Hand write a "PS," if you can. People always read them.

Some rules to break

I hope I've convinced you that breaking rules—where appropriate—is okay. Some grammar rules make no sense even though we were forced to memorize their usage early on. Good writers break rules all the time; they have enough confidence in their writing and their reader to defy the grammar gods.

Here are seven you can break:

1 Use fragments prudently.
We were taught that it was an unforgivable sin to write sentence fragments. Not always! Fragments are incomplete sentences and in certain circumstances work wonderfully. Fragments add interest or give emphasis. Just make certain the fragment relates to the previous sentence or thought. Here is an ad for Cartier:

Cartier. Now at Pacific Place.

Remember—use fragments sparingly and consciously.

2 Use one-sentence paragraphs.
It is a myth that all paragraphs must contain three to five sentences. One-sentence paragraphs can be very effective. Often used in the beginning and ending of memos, they may also be used between long paragraphs as a transition. One-sentence paragraphs exist in text with dialogue and in magazine articles. Check them out.

3 Use inventive words (cautiously).
Inventive words, called *neologisms* (meaning "new words"), can work. New words are created almost daily. Some come from foreign languages (discotheque, pasta) or from technology (software, spamming) or from acronyms (scuba, laser) or are brand names (Xerox, Kleenex). Even nouns are coined as verbs:

Students **seminar** on books they're reading.

Let's **calendar** our next meeting.

In the recent edition of *Webster's College Dictionary*, many *neologisms* were recognized and defined. Here are a few more examples: *digerati* (someone knowledgeable about computers); *stork-parking* (parking for pregnant women); *aquadextrous* (to be able to turn the bathtub faucet on and off with one's toes); *netiquette* (code of courtesy on the Internet). Use neologisms like you would acronyms and jargon—judiciously.

4 Begin sentences with *but, and,* or *because*.
Beginning sentences with the above words can be quite effective when used for emphasis or transition. Here are some good examples:

- And our new Money Market Account offers the best rates in town!

- I understand the difficulty that the imposed timeline has placed on your department. But we must still adhere to our deadline.

- Because of the high crime rate, Mayor Guiliani took extraordinary measures to clean up New York City.
- And he invited fellow citizens to call his new "Quality of Life Hotline" with a toll-free number.

5 Split infinitives.
An infinitive is a verb usually preceded with the word *to*. For example, *to* go; *to* incorporate; *to* agree. Adding an adverb between those two words is just fine: to quickly go; to hurriedly incorporate; to hesitantly agree.

Your own ear remains your best editor. Read what you write out loud to decide whether what you've written makes sense.

Based on the effect the writer wanted to achieve, the following sentence could not be written any other way:

The essence of politics is the art of the con—the ability to convincingly declare that day is night, that up is down, that what is so is not.

6 End with prepositions.
An eighteenth century grammarian insisted that it was more polite not to end sentences with a preposition. Baloney! Use prepositions based on common sense and the tone of the document. I can't resist using this oft-quoted response by Winston Churchill to his editor after being told to discontinue their usage:

This is the sort of English up with which I will not put.

7 Use contractions.
Again the type of document and the reader dictates their use. Technical reports, proposals, and formal letters usually require that you eliminate contractions as they make your writing less formal. However, contractions can make your writing more accessible to the reader. Use them judiciously.

Feedback is the "Breakfast of Champions"

Okay, before you finalize any document, let someone else take a look at it. I cannot stress enough the significance of this step! Letters, memos, reports, brochures, even important e-mails—any writing that will see the light of day—should be read by others before you send it off because—

- Feedback sharpens your final product even though it may drive you crazy, take time, or make you feel like you've bared your soul to the world.

- Feedback does not mean you have to give up your voice or throw out what you've written.

- Feedback is simply getting another perspective—that of the different audiences who will read your document.

- Feedback means that when you hand the document over for review, you ask for specific suggestions from your reader, not just a pat on the back. By getting concrete answers to the questions below, you will be armed with crystal-clear ideas. Also, think about soliciting help from at least two people unlike you in personality.

- Feedback raises the expectation in the organization that words are important and that writing well is a shared goal.

The following are questions you might ask as you go about getting feedback from others:

- ❑ Have I been specific enough?
- ❑ Do I support my ideas with evidence that is objective?
- ❑ Do I present opposing points of view in an objective manner?

❑ Are you able to see the big idea?
❑ Does the document make sense?
❑ Is the document valid, accurate?
❑ Is the organization logical and sequential?
❑ How do you feel as you read this?
❑ Do I have examples that help the reader under-
stand?
❑ Have I made a connection with you, the reader?
❑ Is my writing too detached and impersonal?

Dr. Julie Tip:
Make a feedback sheet with some or all of these
questions. Clip it to your document and circulate.
That way, you will get the feedback you want
rather than ambiguous suggestions or vague praise.

Who you are professionally is mirrored in your writing.
Taking time for feedback can avert the loss of revenue, image,
or clients. A superintendent of a large urban school district
said, "I check my ego at the door and listen intently to the
advice and ideas of others." A CFO of a large hospital con-
curred. "I will always ask others to read my material. The first
question is 'What does this say to you?'"

Quick and Easy Editing

What if you're not looking for comments on the content of your document? Maybe you just want someone to
edit for those tricky grammatical and punctuation errors
that we are all prone to make.

The story of an insurance company that failed to proof
its documents will give you cause to sit up. As the
woeful tale goes, someone in the company wrote a rider
for an existing policy and did not take time to go the extra

mile. Unfortunately, one lonely sentence cost the company hundreds of thousands of dollars, as it read: The company "is liable" rather than, "is not liable."

So how to reduce time when you ask someone to review your document? Pass along a standard editing sheet. The "editor" saves time by not having to write out comments, and the writer saves time through reviewing the editor's shorthand rather than chicken-scratch comments in the margin. Some basic editing marks are below. Just be certain you all agree on them beforehand!

delete material
Be sure to proofread the your document.

spell out
Refer to Chapter 3 for details.

close gap
Zero Power sentences are powerful.

delete material & close gap
You can acquire a lifelong skill.

stet. ignore correction
Who says you can never ever break a rule?

insert letter, word, phrase
You will learn to write quickly.

change letter(s)
Avoid massive voice.

add a space
Getting organized saves you time.

transpose letters/words
Use an easel when working in a group.

Dr. Julie Tip
If you *must* edit your own copy, these guidelines will help polish your document.

Content: Always determine the purpose of your message before you write. Otherwise, your reader will lose interest. Ask yourself: What do you want the reader to do when he/she receives it?

Tone and Style: Write like you talk (See Chapter Three). Picture your reader sitting across from you as you write.

Clarity: Vague words do not add impact. Avoid words with no specificity, like *many, numerous, various, a few.*

Brevity: Every word counts and must have meaning. Be brutal as you edit your writing. Eliminate redundancies and deadwood.

Paragraphs: Avoid reader fatigue: only one topic per paragraph. Make white space your friend.

Conventions: Read your document aloud slowly. Smooth out those awkward or choppy spots. Then read from bottom up to check for spelling, punctuation and grammar.

In Summary

In this chapter you worked hard! Remember you need not practice all the solutions. Some are already in your repertoire. Spend time only on those that feel a little shaky to you.

What's Next

In the next chapter, you will:
- Learn to avoid common business writing flaws.
- Recall punctuation basics.
- Review capitalization guidelines in business.
- Learn how to format your documents correctly.
- Use the guide to chronic misspelling.
- Review guidelines for document design.

And away we go!

CHAPTER FIVE

GET IT WRITE

Prevent Disasters *Before* You Send Your Message!

Over the years, my clients have shared horror stories of the account, the client, the proposal, or the RFP that *got away*. In many cases, it boiled down to neglecting this important step in the writing process—**proofreading**. Poorly placed commas, misspellings, errors in capitalization will cause lost revenue. "We worked three weeks on a huge bid for telephone equipment," said a telecommunications director. "With thirty minutes left, we did not proofread and misspelled the client's name. We lost the bid!"

About two years ago, a wart appeared on my left hand, which I wanted removed.

-Anguished English

Recovering lost revenue is easier than regaining one's reputation. Consider this story:

A young woman, an associate editor in a prestigious magazine, was seeking the next rung up on the career ladder. Discovering her "ideal" job on the Web, she began chatting via e-mail with the human resources director of this company. (*Chatting* is the operative word here.) Because of her informal style, and errors in spelling and punctuation, this woman was never taken seriously nor considered for the position. The human resource director explained it to her in no uncertain terms: "How could we *possibly* hire someone whose writing does not project the professionalism of our organization? Clean up your act, young lady!"

Who you are and what you stand for—your very credibility—is reflected in your documents. *Not* taking the time to make it right is like not combing your hair or dressing appropriately before you meet a client. *Of course* you'd take the time to look your best! Take the same care with your written communication.

You reviewed the C.L.E.V.R. solutions to business writing problems in Chapter Four. They focused on the *content* of your document. Now you need to pay attention to the *details* that can really make or break your professional image. Getting rid of any distracting flaws that may embarrass you, your company, or your boss is the theme of Chapter Five. So . . .

You need to proofread like crazy!

Proofreading can avoid such mistakes as these:

I collided with a stationary truck coming the other way.

I had been driving for forty years when I fell asleep at the wheel and had the accident.

The pedestrian had no idea which direction to turn, so I ran over him.

This chapter is divided into four sections:
- Punctuation
- Capitalization
- Spelling
- Formatting

Each of these makes this point: get it *write* before you send your message!

Dr. Julie Tip:
On very important documents, you might consider reading your writing backwards. Tedious though it may be, this proofreading technique works. By reading backwards, you cause your brain to stop and question "the sense" of your words. Therefore, you have a better chance of catching mistakes.

Punctuation Basics

Most punctuation usage is based on three things: personal choice, consistency, and reader understanding. You need to know the basics.

Periods, exclamation points, and question marks are all straightforward, so let's look at other punctuation perplexities that could make or break you.

The comma

The **comma** is the most widely used and abused of all punctuation marks. Remember these general guidelines:

- Use a comma after a long introductory phrase or clause.

  Contrary to common belief, English women do not wear tweed nightgowns.
  Hermione Gingold

  I've been on so many blind dates, I should get a free dog.
  Wendy Lieberman

- If the introductory phrase is short, no comma is needed:

After the dinner I went home.

- Use a comma to avoid reader confusion. Try reading these sentences out loud without the comma. You'll *hear* the problem.

  Once you understand, the reason is clear.

  If he chooses, Williams can take over the company.

- Use commas to separate a series of items.

  Early to rise and early to bed makes a man healthy, wealthy, and dead.

  Ogden Nash

  The only way to keep your health is to eat what you don't want, drink what you don't like, and do what you'd rather not do.

  Mark Twain

*! In both of these examples, a comma is placed before **and**, which complies with the hard-and-fast rules of punctuation. In everyday writing, however, many people drop the last comma. It's up to you to decide which style to use.*

However, in the examples above, the comma forces the reader to pause and consider the punch line. Another benefit to inserting that last comma is that it can prevent confusion, as in this example:

The farmer has three kinds of cows for sale. They are black, brown and black and brown.

The buyers are probably scratching their heads—how many cows and how many colors? Placing a comma after the first *brown* would quickly clear up this mystery.

- Use a comma to separate complete sentences that are joined with a conjunction: *and, but, for, or, nor, yet,* or *so.*

*The optimist proclaims that we live in the best of all possible times, **and** the pessimist fears this is true.*
James Branch Cabell
*Everybody talks about the weather, **but** nobody does anything about it.*
Mark Twain

- Use commas to separate nonessential phrases from the rest of the sentence. The words between the commas may be deleted, and the sentence still makes sense.

  Unlike Andy Rooney, who puts out a book every year, I at least have the courtesy to wait two years before I offer something new.
  Art Buchwald
  Pessimism, when you get used to it, is just as agreeable as optimism.
  Arnold Bennett

- Use a comma when you are directly addressing someone.

  Reader, suppose you were an idiot. And suppose you are a member of Congress. But I repeat myself.
  Mark Twain
  Dr. Livingstone, I presume?
  Sir Henry Morton Stanley

- Use a comma between a proper name and a title or explanatory phrase, known as an appositive. Appositives are words that follow nouns or phrases and give more information. They, like parenthetical phrases, are not necessary for the sentence to make sense, but are informative to the reader.

  Bill Gates, Chief Software Architect, spoke in Las Vegas last month.

> *My son, the orthodontist, sent me flowers for my birthday.*
>
> *Let us be grateful to Adam, our benefactor. He cut us out of the "blessing" of idleness and won for us the "curse" of labor.*
>
> Mark Twain

- Use commas to separate items in a geographical address.

  Positano, Italy

  10 Glandore, Dalkey, County Dublin, Eire

- Use commas with quoted material.

  "Nothing is so admirable in politics as a short memory," said John Kenneth Galbraith.

- *Do not* use commas to separate the subject of the sentence from the verb.

  Wrong: Upfront discussions, save a lot of grief.

  Right: Upfront discussions save a lot of grief.

This can also cause misunderstanding when a long phrase occurs before the verb.

Wrong: Traveling, reading, and gardening, are my three favorite pastimes.

Right: Traveling, reading, and gardening are my three favorite pastimes.

Remember, the technique of putting a comma where you naturally pause is okay *most of the time.* The above basics will help you with the rest of the time.

The colon

The **colon** is used to alert the reader. It gives a signal: *Okay here comes information.* It introduces a list or a quote or an explanation. It takes the place of the words *that is* or *for example*. The colon is also sometimes used to open a business letter when you do not know the recipient.

In two words: im possible.

Samuel Goldwyn

Zsa Zsa Gabor once observed: "I am a very good house-keeper. Each time I get divorced I keep the house."

On a divorce lawyer's wall: Satisfaction guaranteed or your honey back.

Dear Sir or Madam:

* Use a colon after *as follows* or *following*.

   The ingredients of a diplomat's life have been identi-fied as follows: protocol, alcohol, and Geritol.

The semicolon

The **semicolon** is the odd duck in the world of punctuation. It's neither a period nor a comma, but a little bit of both. More formal than the colon or the dash, it forces the reader to pause.

A semicolon separates two main clauses, each forming a complete thought. Since the clauses are closely related, they are better joined together with a semicolon. Using *and* or a period would not have the same impact.

Old grammarians never die—they just lose their verb and slip into a comma.

-Get Thee to a Punnery

When angry, count four; when very angry, swear.

Mark Twain

In politics, if you want anything said, ask a man; if you want anything done, ask a woman.

Margaret Thatcher

Freedom is never voluntarily given by the oppressor; it must be demanded by the oppressed.

Martin Luther King, Jr.

Semicolons can also be used to:
- Separate a list of complex items:

Persons attempting to find a motive in this narrative will be prosecuted; persons attempting to find a moral in it will be banished; persons attempting to find a plot will be shot.

Mark Twain

- To separate clauses that have commas:

At my fiftieth birthday party, the caterer prepared a vegetable basket with two dips, ranch and dried tomato; assorted imported cheeses, including Gruyère and brie; a fresh shellfish bar with clams, oysters, and scallops; a pasta bar with six sauces; and three different desserts.

The dash

The **dash** can be a dramatic tool *if* used sparingly. If used too often, it can be a distraction. A dash says to the reader abruptly, *I'm now going to make a strong statement—one that I want you to pay attention to.* It places additional emphasis on an idea and can be used like a comma, colon, or parentheses. You are hereby officially warned about its misuse.

It's not the men in your life that count—it's the life in your man.

Mae West

A classic—something that everybody wants to have read and nobody wants to read.

Mark Twain

I think—therefore I'm single.

Lizz Winstead

*Some word-processing programs turn two hyphens into a **long dash** (—) (called an em dash because it's the length of a capital M) if you type them together. Otherwise, always use two hyphens. You decide; just be consistent.*

Parentheses

Parentheses are even *less* formal marks than the dash. They mean to be an aside, something that you would whisper to the reader. They make the reader pause so that you can tell them something chatty, interesting, or helpful *but* not essential to your document. If you don't care whether the reader pays attention to the information in the **parentheses**—fine. If you do care—don't use them. Your sentence should make sense even if the information in the parentheses were to be deleted.

> *For God's sake don't make me ridiculous any more by terming me gentle-hearted in print. (I never was more serious.)*
> Charles Lamb

> *My old grannum (rest her soul) was wont to say, there were but two families in the world, have-much and have-little.*
> Miguel De Cervantes

Punctuate material enclosed in the parentheses when it occurs outside the main sentence. (See the first example above.)

Quotation marks

Quotation marks are mostly used just as their name suggests: to show the reader what was said "exactly." They can add interest, variety, or credibility to your document.

> *When someone exultantly exclaimed, "Eureka!" Chico Marx shot back, "You donna smella so good yourself!"*

> *"No, Eve, I won't touch that apple," said Tom adamantly.*

Other uses of quotation marks are:

- To enclose a word or phrase that is being defined:

  The two most beautiful words in the English language are "Check enclosed."
  Dorothy Parker

- For words with special meaning:

  "Idea Maps" can help you quickly organize your conference speech.

- To identify titles of articles, essays, poems, short stories, songs, or chapters.

  "Five Indispensable Time Management Habits"

Italics

Thanks to the shift from typewriter to computer, the use of **italics** has gained popularity. Where once you underlined, now italics are used. Italics show emphasis, signify titles, or identify foreign words that are not readily recognized by the reader.

- Italicize titles of books, periodicals, newspapers, movies, paintings, television shows, plays, magazines, long poems, works of art, ships, trains, and aircraft.

The Wall Street Journal	*The Honeymooners*
Carmen	*Crossing to Safety*
The Concorde	*The Thinker*

- Italicize unfamiliar foreign words.

  Our exchange student from Italy used the word *andiamo* which means "let's go!"

- Italicize for emphasis.

  I *really* don't want to go.

Apostrophe

The much-maligned **apostrophe** gets as much abuse as the comma. The confusion seems to be mostly around possessive nouns and contractions.

- Use an apostrophe to signify ownership/possession:

  The manager's paycheck = the paycheck belongs to the manager

  Writer's block = the block belongs to the writer

- Use an apostrophe only for plural possessives when the noun ends with an s:

  Garbage drivers' strike

  Engineers' new salaries

- Use apostrophes to signify contractions, where two words are combined to make one and a letter or letters are dropped. For example: it's = it is. The apostrophe takes the place of the letter *i*. If you find it easy to make this mistake, just read the word as if it's (it is) two words. *Its* is a possessive. **It's important to know the distinction between these two.**

  One frog to another:
  Time's fun when
  you're having flies.
  -Get Thee to a
  Punnery

Some everyday contractions:

I'm=I am	*can't= cannot*
I'll=I will	*doesn't=does not*
I've=I have	*they've=they have*
isn't=is not	*s/he's=s/he is*

aren't= are not   you've= you have

I've been called many things, but never an intellectual.
Tallulah Bankhead

Remember possessive pronouns **do not** use a contraction: Hers, his, its, theirs, ours, yours, whose.

Life is for each man a solitary cell whose walls are mirrors.
Eugene O'Neill

- Use apostrophes to show omission of one or more letters in a word or a number:

Th' only way t' entertain some folks is t' listen t' 'em.
Kim Hubbard

Class reunion of '95 (1995)

When you use contractions, consider the reader, your purpose, and the accepted practices of your organization. Always determine appropriateness.

! Since deciding where to put apostrophes makes most of us crazy, Gregg's Reference Manual, *mentioned in Chapter Three, will come in handy.*

Hyphens

The **hyphen** is most often used to join compound words that have a relationship with each other: brother-in-law; self-love; editor-in-chief. Hyphens can also clear up misunderstandings. For example, hyphens would have helped in these headlines:

Eye drops off shelf
British Left waffles on Falklands
Squad helps dog bite victim.

Hyphens are used for compound numbers from twenty-one to ninety-nine. Hyphens also occur after these prefixes: self, ex, all.

If prefixes used for a common element are listed in a sentence, insert a suspending hyphen.

The teenage girls pranced in front of the mirrors in their maxi-, midi-, and miniskirts.

Take out an 8 1/2- by 11-inch piece of paper.

Capitalization

As with punctuation, you already know the basics to capitalization. Just as a reminder, I have listed persons, places and things that need to be capitalized. Check those reference books for additional specifics.

Capitalize the following:

- Names and initials for persons
  Anthony E. Smith
  Dr. Mary Lynne Derrington

- Places, geographical areas
  San Marino, California
  Europe
  the South

- Organizations and their members, corporations, government agencies
  Dept. of Corrections   Junior League   Rotarians

- Ships, planes, and spacecraft
  The Crystal Harmony   Voyager II

- Ethnic groups, races, religions, languages
  Jewish   Italian   Muslim   Farsi

- Days, months, holidays, historical periods/events
  Monday   August   Fourth of July
  Boston Tea Party   President's Day

- First word in a quote
  *Humorous writer, Dorothy Parker, said in a theatre review, "**She** runs the gamut of emotions from A to B."*
- Book titles, articles, plays, films, reports, poems, works of art, musical compositions
  Business Writing That Counts!   Les Miserables Saving Private Ryan   The Pietà   La Bohème
- Trade names
  Band-Aid   Coca Cola   Q-Tip   Windows 2000

Spelling

Spelling can intimidate even the best of us, as rules, and exceptions to those rules, abound. Fortunately, most word processing software has spell-check. *That,* as you know, *does not* excuse you from proofing your document before it goes out! Misspelled words can project a poor image or inaccurate information. Peruse these dillies:

The choir will meet at the Larsen home for fun and sinning.

Save regularly at our bank. You'll never reget it.

Misspelled words can also cause confusion as in these sets of words: *stationery* or *stationary; principle* or *principal; affect* or *effect.*

Two suggestions to help you with your spelling:

1 **Keep that dictionary close to your computer.** If you don't know how to spell the word that you want to look up, think of a synonym for that word.

2 **Keep a list of words that you frequently misspell.** You might even try to memorize them. For example, the word "stationery" (materials for writing or typing) is really tough for me to remember. So I memorized it by relating it to the

word pap*er*. The *er* at the end is my clue to
its spelling.

Here is a list of some commonly misspelled words:

accept/except	conference	fortunate
accommodate	confidential	generally
achieve	congratulate	government
acknowledge	consequence	grammar
adjustment	consensus	guarantee
advertisement	continuous	guess
advice	convenience	hazardous
agreement	courteous	height
allotted	courtesy	hoping
all right	customer	identical
answer	decision	illegible
appointment	definitely	immediately
appreciate	dependent	inconvenience
assignment	development	individual
assistant	dilemma	inquiry
authority	dissatisfied	instead
balance	doubt	Internet
bargain	e-commerce	interrupt
beneficial	economical	knowledge
brochure	efficiency	language
budget	eliminate	liability
business	e-mail	library
calendar	embarrass	license
catalog	emphasize	listen
certain	enough	maintenance
challenge	enthusiastic	making
circumstance	especially	mayor
clientele	excellent	meant
color	experience	mileage
commercial	facilities	miscellaneous
commission	February	misspell
committed	finally	monotonous
competition	foreign	mortgage

necessary	professor	thorough
negotiate	realize	though
noticeable	really	tomorrow
oblige	receipt	truly
occasion	receive	unfortunately
occurrence	recommend	unique
opportunity	reimburse	unnecessary
original	respectfully	usable
pamphlet	ridiculous	useful
participant	salary	usually
particularly	satisfactory	vague
patience	Saturday	various
permanent	secretary	Web site
personnel	separate	Wednesday
persuade	sincerely	writing
possible	sufficient	written
practically	technique	yesterday
preferred	temporary	
procedure	their	

Formatting

Formatting your document is a proofreading necessity. Your document needs to be as easy on your readers' eyes as your words are on their ears. Being able to quickly scan a document tops most readers' lists. Conversely, if readers have to plow through dense text, your document will surely be put at the bottom of the pile. Don't make it too tough and time-consuming to get through your words! So visually lay out your text so that it is visually attractive and is appropriate for the purpose of the document. I promise you will win immediate friends.

Headings, white space, lists, font style, graphs, and charts aid readers in understanding.

According to Peggy Jacobson, Ph.D., owner of TCCI (www.tccink.com), a Seattle-based technical and instructional design company, consider these techniques when formatting your documents.

Guidelines for document design

Page Design

- Use multiple-level headings to show organization. Use larger, bolder type for more important headings. Make them task- or reader-oriented. For example, use: *Applications for Low Income Housing* rather than *Applications.*
- Chunk information in short blocks to allow readers to scan it easily. Use white space or page breaks to group related information. Create vertical or horizontal spaces that aid in laying out a manual, brochure, or newsletter.
- Use text boxes to create special elements for page design and draw attention to key information.
- Use wide margins, keeping your line length to five inches or less.
- Use ragged right-hand margins to increase reading comprehension. Research has shown that ragged right-hand margins help readers process information more quickly.

Typography

- Use ALL CAPITALS very sparingly. Small Caps are nice. Reserve capitals for text elements that deserve unusual attention.
- Use bold or italics for emphasis, but use sparingly.
- Don't overuse exclamation marks and underlines. Be angry!, or perhaps *angry*, but not angry!!!
- Underlining, particularly on Web pages, can cause confusion because hypertext links are typically underlined.
- Use numbered or bulleted paragraphs and lists to highlight important information. Use numbers

only when the order of the task or idea is important.

- Use tables for easy access to information.
- Limit information to no more than five to seven items at a time. Studies have shown people cannot keep track of more than seven pieces of information.
- Font size and style: For ease of reading, consider using a sans serif font (e.g., Times Roman) and consider your audience. Over 40 year olds like 12 point font.
- Use templates and apply styles for consistency and to save time. Create your own look and feel for a standard report, newsletter, or e-mail blast. Readers will recognize it the minute they see it and want to read what you have to say.

Chunk Information

You can organize information for users by dividing it into manageable chunks, both conceptually and visually.

- Group information in short blocks, rather than burying the content in long paragraphs and sections.
- Use highlighting devices to direct the reader's eye and create emphasis. Typographic devices (boldface, italics, shading), rules, and boxes can distinguish items in a text, emphasize a specific section, and help the reader locate main sections.
- Try text-boxes, pulled-quotes, or abstracts. Magazines use this trick to draw readers' eyes to a point of interest in a high-profile way. By putting short attention grabbers in the margin or in a separate graphic element, you can entice your readers to read the full information in the adjacent column or paragraph.

Use of Color

Only use color if you know what you are doing. Color used to jazz up a document may not add anything at all.

- Accomplish specific goals with color (to warn or caution, for instance).
- Communicate, don't decorate. Resist the urge to add stationary to e-mail unless the theme is pertinent to your message.
- Be careful with color-coding in spreadsheets or other reports. Readers may be colorblind. They may also print the spreadsheets on a black and white office printer and lose the meaning.
- Prioritize information with color. Readers will go to bright colors first.
- Symbolize with color. Draw on your knowledge of your readers.
- Identify a theme that recurs or sequence information with color.
- Code different symbols or sections with color to make searching for information easier.

In Summary

I explained how to prevent disasters before you send your message and provided invaluable formatting guidance for all your communication. Having pride in your work requires paying attention to details. Those details are important whether you're writing an eighty-page report or a one-page summary. I encouraged you to purchase a reference handbook for punctuation, spelling, and capitalization specifics not covered in this section. Lots of sources are available online or in books.

What's Next

In the next chapter, you will learn:
- Tips for memos that get read.
- The basics of a business letter.
- The do's and don'ts of letter writing.
- Effective models for good and bad newsletters.
- The elements of a successful sales letter.
- How to organize PR letters and news releases.
- How to write thank-you and acceptance letters.
- An easy format for business proposals and reports.
- Examine electronic communications.
- Use the six tips for sending professional faxes.

Hi ho, hi ho, it's off to work we go!

Chapter Six

Get Writing

Have Templates, Save Time

In the previous chapters, I hope you have been empowered, encouraged, and educated by the information I have presented. Chapter Six can be your reference guide for those common and not-so-common writing tasks:

- Letters
- Press Releases
- Professional Reports
- Proposals
- Executive Summaries
- E-mails

I write at high speed because boredom is bad for my health. It upsets my stomach more than anything else. I also avoid green vegetables. They're grossly overrated.

-Noel Coward

In the following pages, you will see templates for your everyday kinds of communication along with examples (sometimes written tongue in cheek). And, yes, yes, I know that most of these types of correspondence are occurring online, but you still need to remember the basics!

Since one of the recurring themes is saving time, I won't disappoint in this chapter. Developing good models for frequent topics makes good sense. Just be certain that you personalize them.

> Dr. Julie Tip:
> When asked to review a company's letter templates, I always advise that they keep them fresh by reviewing, rewriting, and/or tossing out the old ones. How often? About every four to six months.

Memos

Memos certainly are the most widely used form of communication within an organization. Standard requirements for memos? Keep them concise and to the point. The e-mail writing guidelines in this chapter apply to memos as well. These nine important tips will ensure your message gets read!

1   **Make memos clear, organized, and credible.** Judgments about you will be made based on these semiformal pieces of writing.

2   **Keep memos short and sweet.** Strive for an average of 12-15 words per sentence. Use the one-'n-one rule: one main point in one page.

3   **Save your reader time.** Like with e-mail, the subject line—usually just a phrase—should be as specific as possible. It functions the same way as a report title.

4   **Begin with a statement of the memo's main idea (remember Power 1?).** Be direct and to the point. State the purpose in the opening sentence.

5 **Position your ideas; the most important goes first, followed by the next most important.** You can highlight your points with bullets or asterisks.

6 **Be clear about what you want the reader to do with the information in your memo.** Dates, details, and deadlines all help get a timely response, if one is required.

7 *Do* **send a memo when you want to:**

- Protect your idea within the organization
- Formally state your opinion regarding a decision
- Make a request
- Confirm a decision
- Praise someone for work well done

8 *Don't* **send a memo if you have *any* doubts.** Pick up the phone or walk down the hall. Memos have a *very long* shelf life.

9 **Open with a positive statement.** Then, if you have to, present the bad news and close with a possible solution or different perspective.

Letters

Letters endure as probably the oldest form of business communication, whether sent snail mail or electronically. They are written primarily to inform (with good or bad news) or to persuade. Moreover, they represent *you* and your organization. Using a basic letter format is a necessary detail in your correspondence. A quick review of the standard parts to a business letter plus a list of dos and don'ts follows.

Parts of a business letter

Mr. Edward Fitzpatrick
1143 West Diamond Street
Butte, MT 98072-2222
December 31, 1999

Heading: Gives the complete address of the sender with no abbreviations (or have all information on letterhead). You may either spell out the name of the state or use U.S. Postal Service abbreviations.

Chris Wall
Producer
Wrangler Rhythm Records
7416 Towne Avenue
Los Angeles, CA 91724-2222

Inside address: Put the name of person to whom you are writing— first name/initial, last name— followed by the title, company name, and address on separate lines. Double-check that all are spelled correctly.

Dear Mr. Wall:

Salutation: Be careful that you address the person correctly: Mr., Ms., Dr., Superintendent, etc. A colon is generally used after the salutation, but a comma may be used if you know the person and its use seems appropriate.

We would like to invite . . .
you will be welcome to . . .
and the rest of these . . .
on the first of the . . .

Beginning and Body: Be sure you have an effective opening sentence. Make that first paragraph positive and informative. (Chapter Three) You can use bullets, numbers, or lists to help your reader. Elaboration on your main point(s) occurs here with Power 2's and 3's. (Chapter Two)

Excuse me for not answering your letter, but I've been so busy not answering letters that I couldn't get around to not answering yours in time.

-Groucho Marx

Therefore, if you will . . .
so we may confirm all the . . .
make the final arrangements . . .
We would like to have . . .
as soon as it is . . .

Ending: As important as the opening
sentences are, your ending (Chapter
Three) lets your reader know what he/
she should do next and/or creates
goodwill. Enclosures, attachments,
forms are mentioned here, as well as
follow-up information.

Sincerely,

Complimentary closing: Type this two line
spaces below the ending of the body.
Standard expressions are *Sincerely* or
Sincerely yours. After a relationship with
reader has formed perhaps try: *Regards*,
or *Cordially*. Always place a comma after
this closing.

Ed Fitzpatrick

Your signature: Sign your name here. It
can differ from the typed professional
name that will follow your signature. Again,
if you have a relationship with the recipient,
perhaps sign the letter just with your first
name. It's your call.

Edward Fitzpatrick
Attorney-at-Law

Full name and business title on
separate lines.

EF/jp

Reference initials of the person who wrote
letter (caps) followed by initials of the person
who typed letter (lower case).

Enclosure

Enclosure notation: If additional material is
enclosed, it can be indicated by *Enc.*,
Enclosure, or *Enclosure*, followed by name
of enclosed item, e.g., book invoices.

C: P. Beisser
    L. Chenok
    L. Miller
    B. Moore

Copy notations: C, which stands for copy,
has replaced CC. Indicate, in alphabetical
order, to whom the copies have been sent.

Letter Dos and Don'ts

Do:

❑ Follow the concepts and strategies presented in this book as you organize, begin, and write your letter. Be correct in every detail.

❑ Use either full block style or left justified with ragged right (less formal but easier on the eye). These are the most common formats. All text stays to the left with no indentation at the beginning of the paragraphs. Double-space between paragraphs.

❑ Determine where to put "good" or "bad" news in your letter. It should be based on circumstances, the reader, and the purpose.

❑ Call the reader by name, if appropriate.

❑ Tell the reader what you can do and/or what should happen next.

❑ Develop letter templates or models. Yes, it's important to consider your reader, but having a boilerplate model on hand that can be personalized will save you time, especially if you are sending out the same letter to a number of clients.

Don't:

❑ Start "bad news" letters with the bad news. Put a buffer sentence first before you disappoint or anger your reader.

❑ Manipulate your reader, put on airs, be cute, or exaggerate. S/he won't be fooled.

No one can write decently who is distrustful of the reader's intelligence or whose attitude is patronizing.

-E.B. White

❑ Use canned beginnings (*Enclosed please find…*) or endings (*Call me if you're interested…*). (See Chapter Three)

❑ Summarize your points at the end unless it's a long letter.
❑ Feel the necessity to use all the letter details presented above. Your audience and purpose will determine what you include.

Letter Templates

This section presents usable templates or patterns for the most common types of letters.

The "good news" letter

At least half of all business letters contain a positive message. From responding to an inquiry about your product or service, to filling an order, to making an adjustment, to extending credit, to sending congratulations, they all contain information the reader is interested in receiving. These letters have a similar format:

Beginning: State the good, most important news enthusiastically, if appropriate.

Body: Give any necessary details (perhaps a sales pitch for your product).

I have made this letter longer than usual because I lack the time to make it shorter.

-Blaise Pascal

Ending: Close with a cordial, courteous comment that creates goodwill and shows appreciation for the person's business.

This letter sends congratulations to a customer:

Dear Ms. Hart:

Congratulations on winning the Podunk lottery! We are happy to increase your advance line to $200,000. Please *come into the bank to sign the documents by October 16th. Included with the advance line increase you will have: unlimited check writing; a free bankcard; a free safe deposit box; free traveler's checks; plus we will waive the first year's annual fee on your platinum credit card.*

Also, be sure to bring the certificate with you so that we can assist you in securing this advance line. We thank you for your continued business with ABC Bank and look forward to meeting all your future banking needs.

Let my receptionist know when you come in, as I would like to meet you! Or feel free to call me at 555-XXXX and set up an appointment time. I have some exciting new programs to share for special customers like you.

Sincerely,
Mallory Miles

The "bad news" letter

Letters that contain a negative message are neither pleasant to write nor to receive. The **"bad news"** letter may respond to a customer complaint, refuse a claim, reject an applicant, or decline an invitation. Because you may disappoint (even anger) the receiver, consideration should be extended to your reader. Put yourself in the reader's shoes as you compose this letter. Maintaining goodwill while not further antagonizing the reader should be your goal:

Beginning: Start with a buffer statement. You want to create a friendly, positive tone.

Advice is judged by results, not by intentions.

    -Cicero

Body: Include a logical explanation for your negative news. Review the facts and circumstances surrounding the decision. Details should be included only if no legal ramifications could occur. You are not always obligated to justify your "no." Focus on the *thing* not the person. If possible, state the situation in a positive (Refer to page 117) rather than negative form. For example, instead of writing: *You did not send the correct form*, try *Please send the correct form*.

Ending: Close with anything positive about the situation. Offer a friendly suggestion, wish the reader future success, or present a reasonable alternative.

A familiar letter to most of us:

Dear Tony,

Thank you so much for your time and interest regarding the division manager position. You have many impressive qualities, which made the final choice a tough decision for our interview team.

Though all three of our finalists were excellent, we have hired a candidate whose qualifications best fit the position at this time.

Thank you for your interest in our company. I wish you much success in your future endeavors.

Best regards,
Christian Carter

The complaint or claims letter

This section is includes two kinds of letters: correcting and rejecting.

This first type of letter is written about a situation that needs *correcting*. Always treat your customer with respect no matter the circumstances. You might want to mention the service you have provided in the past and will continue to do so in the future. Here the customer's request or claim is turned down.

Beginning: Thank the reader for notifying you. Use facts, dates, places, people, numbers, cost, etc., as appropriate.

Body: Explain clearly and logically what will be done. State sequentially why the incident occurred. Suggest alternatives if appropriate.

Ending: Close with an apology for any inconvenience or confusion that may have been caused. Maintaining good customer relations is important, so include a phone number for the recipient.

This letter *rejects* a customer's claim:

Dear Mr. Matthew Burn:

Thank you for your letter concerning the replacement of your Merry Widow microwave model #12345. We have reviewed your request.

Your letter stated that after mounting it on top of your station wagon, it quit working within a week. Since Merry Widows are not designed for outdoor usage, especially during our rainy season, we cannot honor your request for a new microwave. The warranty does not extend to outdoor use. I have enclosed another copy of the instruction manual for future reference.

Please come in to our showroom soon to see our latest models—on sale! We have an excellent product line of microwaves for indoor use. If you have any further questions, please call our Customer Service Department at 555-XXXX.

Sincerely,
Angela Adams

The "customer is always right" theory seems to work best as you think about your response. The tone of your letter is essential. Be courteous and positive. Here the customer's complaint is addressed.

Beginning: Start with the "good news" and apologize for the error. Show that you understand.

Body: Explain logically what went wrong or what caused the problem. Also let the reader know how you plan to resolve the issue.

Ending: Show appreciation for the reader's business. Close with a pleasant, future-oriented sentence.

This letter corrects a customer's complaint:

Dear Dr. Browne:

Thank you for notifying us about your long wait at the drive-up window on May 8th. Twelve minutes is too much time to wait for service.

On that day only one teller was working the drive-up, our staff having been temporarily reduced by the recent influenza epidemic. Our tellers are all well now, so the situation should not occur again.

In the future, if you are pressed for time, our ATM machine could be a good alternative. We would be happy to order a card for you if you don't have one. For your convenience, I have enclosed an application.

Illiterate?
Write today for
free help!
  ‐Anguished English

First State bank is committed to providing top quality customer service. We hope your next opportunity to use our drive-up window is problem free. Please call me if you have further questions or comments at 555-XXXX.

Sincerely,
Eamonn Edwards

Enc.

The sales letter

Sales letters are always about trying to *persuade* the reader to buy a product or service. The reader does not always view them with great fondness, so enthusiasm (voice) for your business must come through. The reader is interested only if your **product or service directly benefits him/her**. Therefore, you must get to the point quickly, directly, *and* in an interesting way. In the next section you will learn in more detail sales-writing concepts. Here I give you the basics.

Beginning: Hook your reader (remember Zero Power?) with an idea or an offer. You have great news: your product or service. Create interest by appealing to the reader's desire to gain prestige or approval or more income; to a sense of compassion; to a desire to become happier; to the reader's curiosity; or to that universal urge to get something free.

Knowing your audience has never been more important! Downplay the use of *I, me, mine, my, we, our, ours,* and *us* and emphasize *you, your,* and *yours.* Whether or not you know the recipient personally will determine the first sentence.

Doing business without advertising is like winking at a girl in the dark; you know what you're doing, but nobody else does.

-S. Britt

Body: Sell your product or service with convincing facts, figures, statistics, or anything that provides proof of the outstanding qualities of your product/service. Testimonials, endorsements, personal stories, or a limited free or reduced offer are all ways to appeal to your reader. You want to create a favorable impression of your product. Perhaps you will include brochures or pictures with your letter. Bullets or lists help the reader scan your information.

Ending: Ask your reader to do something: *call, write, send money, drive over,* or *go online.* Here you want to make it as convenient as possible for your reader to act immediately. This is a sales technique where you combine benefits with goodwill. You may—depending on purpose, audience, and circumstances—want to apply pressure by asking a question or spurring action with a deadline.

If you have trouble constructing a letter, create an Idea Map first! Mapping question: *What major features of my company/product/services will benefit my customer/client?* Once you come up with a word or phrase, put it in the middle of your Idea Map...OR use this sentence below as a guide:

My product/service

(Describe here in detail)

has these features

(List every feature you can think of)

that benefit my customer in these ways.

(How will your product/service help your customer/client?)

Think about the advantages or strengths of your product/service. You need to explain/describe the benefits to your reader. You also need to think about what objections your reader might have to the product, and then find ways to address these concerns.

This is a sales letter to a customer after initial contact had been made:

Dear Ms. Bethel:

It was great meeting with you this week. Did I mention that our company could provide accounting services that will increase your bottom line by $2 million annually? Our ability to manage your accounts will free up your time so that you can create an even larger client base.

Goldcoin Accounting will quickly and easily set up a system in your organization that can accomplish increased profitability and morale. First, we will streamline your accounting system. We guarantee a 20 percent (minimum!) increase in gross profits the first year. Second, to introduce our new partnership, we will put on a company picnic like you've never seen before. Talk about raising employee morale!

We know the needs of businesses like yours because we have firsthand experience in what it takes to manage a business. Enclosed is a client list—feel free to contact any of them. Also, we have sent along our company brochure giving you more detailed information. I look forward to our meeting next Thursday at 10 a.m. Please feel free to call my office if you have questions before then.

Sincerely,

Mark Connoy

Mark Connoy
President and CEO

PS: This 10% discount coupon is good for your first month with us!

Dr. Julie Tip:
Evaluate your online sales communications, too! Since Internet users can visit lots of competing Web sites before they make a purchase, you must create carefully crafted, benefit-oriented online sales messages that convince prospects you have a solution to their problem. Nancy J. Wagner, founder of *Cut to the Chase Marketing* (www.cuttothechase marketing.com) offers these suggestions to help you refine your online messages:

- Know your reader. Who is your target market? What do they need to know about your products and services to convince them to buy? Create problem/ solution or benefit-oriented copy and headlines that answer these questions.

- Determine the real goal of your Web site. Is it to make a sale online or to encourage prospects to contact you for more information? Make every word count towards your expected outcome.

- Create a warm, friendly online message. Your Web site copy should sound like you're talking to the reader in person. Since your Web site has to work in your absence, make sure it feels honest, inviting, and interesting.

- Use courteous, friendly language when replying to prospect e-mails. Your e-mail response should show your willingness to provide excellent customer service. This helps convince prospects that you'll also be helpful after the sales process—a big plus when they decide to buy!

- Ask acquaintances to give you feedback about your Web site and reply e-mail messages. After reviewing both your Web site and reply e-mails, ask yourself: would they buy or not? If they hesitate before buying, find out why, then change your Web site or e-mail messages accordingly.

The thank-you letter

This time-honored letter has gone sadly and increasingly out of style. People no longer take the time to thank others, but it remains a powerful (let alone courteous) sales and marketing tool *and* puts you above the crowd. Thanking a client for his or her account, showing appreciation to a friend for a referral, or just saying you enjoyed meeting someone spells *first rate*. You'll be remembered even more if you personalize it by adding details rather than just sending the generic form letter. The **thank-you letter** does not have to be long; four or five sentences will suffice. It's the thought that counts.

Beginning: Thank the reader in the first sentence for the specific act.

Body *(can be part of opening paragraph)*: Mention why you are thanking them with specific comments.

Ending: Close with the next steps you will take (if appropriate) or a breezy goodwill statement.

! *If you handwrite your letter, it's even classier!*

Dear Jeff,

Thank you so much for giving me the opportunity to present the Business Writing That Counts! *training to your employees last week. They were a wonderful group and seemed to enjoy the exercises in my book. Your department heads said that the Power Numbers system was an easy tool for them to use in organizing their year-end report.*

Thank you again. I look forward to our continued relationship.

Sincerely,
Ryan Roberts

Press Releases

These documents contain information that you want to get out to the media, such as newspapers, TV and radio stations. **Press Releases** can be announcements about management promotions, year-end financial reports, fund-raising efforts, etc., or they might just be a component of your larger press kit.
Press releases have a definite format.

Beginning: Start with a Zero Power sentence that generates excitement, enthusiasm, and interest in your news. Don't forget to include the five W's (who, what, where, when, why) and the H (how) within the first paragraph. According to Candace Kovner Bel Air, a media consultant in Seattle, TV stations in major markets receive one hundred press releases a day! So using words such as *first, last, new, unique, one-of-a-kind, only, different* will cause yours to stand out.

Body: Include the facts with details about the organization, event, business, or product. These may be changes in management, a new acquisition or product, or a public service announcement (PSA). If the release is about your business, include any positive attributes/benefits of your product/service in order of importance. If appropriate, use a celebrity endorsement or a quote from a happy customer.

Conclusion: Be brief, listing any pertinent information the reader may need. If you include a sales pitch, it goes here, but create a clear and simple description.

FOR IMMEDIATE RELEASE

Contact: Ann Hill
744 Carly Ave
Whittier, CA 98111-2222 (210) 475-1234

NEW BOOK HELPS BUSINESS WRITERS QUIT CIRCLING THE COMPUTER!

SOMERVILLE, NJ—Business Writing That Counts! *introduces a unique approach—organizing with numbers— to those who have to write in their work world. This entertaining and informative book presents readers with fast and effective ways to get started, get organized, and get writing.*

"By using my numbering system, you can cut your writing time in half," said Dr. Julie Miller, author of Business Writing That Counts! *"After years of working with people and their issues around writing, I finally decided to write down*

what I'd been advising." She added that finding a way to "quit circling the computer and get writing" is important to her clients. "Time is always a critical factor." Miller consults with individual clients as well as conducts training seminars. She estimates that she has presented this system to over a million people nationwide.

Dr. Miller's book assists the full spectrum of writers. Whether they write the occasional memo or develop formal reports, Business Writing That Counts! *provides invaluable techniques and strategies for completing a writing task and getting the message out. Additionally, a special section is devoted exclusively to sales writing with tools to help writers produce communication that sells.*

What distinguishes this book from other business writing books? "I've made mine very user-friendly. Writing is intimidating enough for most people," says Miller. "Why scare them to death? My contention is you can break a few rules and still produce a powerful document."

Dr. Miller's Web site offers additional writing strategies (www.businesswritingthatcounts.com). "Yes, I wanted to have a place where people can get help for their ordinary as well extraordinary writing tasks."

###

Professional Reports

Documents longer than two or three pages that present information so the reader(s) can make a decision may become **reports**. I have included a three-step process—designing, developing, drafting—for writing a formal report. As always, your reader and the *report requirements* will determine what to include.

Design the report

1 **Determine your reader: primary (usually the decision makers) and secondary (any others who will read the report).** Consider your reader's concerns, needs, and issues. Check out the *Reader Meter* in the Appendix; review past chapters that discuss the reader. Will you have a sales component to this report? If so, what are the benefits?

2 **Idea Map the reader's key questions regarding your topic.**

3 **Pinpoint the one question that stands out as the *most important.*** That's the one you'll answer in the report.

4 **Group the related reader questions to create report sections.** For example, related reader question: *When will the project be completed?* Report section title: *Expected Completion Date.*

Develop the content

- Summarize each reader question under a report section.
- Write summary statements under each section.
- Introduce details gathered from research and data.
- Create section headings and subheadings, using two to three per page.

Draft the content

1 **Flesh out the summary statement.** Present your information logically. Adddress specifics that detail the major and minor issues. Use the Power Numbers.

2 **Build on your summary statements,** adding visual aids to make your information user-friendly:
- White space
- Bullets, lists or numbers
- Graphics, visuals, illustrations, graphs, tables, organizational or flow charts (careful here—don't want to overwhelm the reader)
- Capital letters, bolded words, underlining, italics, or various fonts

3 **Write the conclusion.** As an important part of the report (usually read right after the summary), it ties up loose ends and:
- Restates the purpose of the document
- Draws conclusions
- Makes recommendations
- Interprets findings or research
- Presents results

Be certain that your conclusion and your introduction match. Did the report deliver what you said it would in your introduction? Whatever you wrote in the beginning of the document must be addressed in the conclusion. Sometimes an implementation process is introduced along with a timeline, including the details about cost, personnel, and time commitment.

4 **Write your executive summary/introduction/ abstract.**

5 **Revise, revise, revise!** Review all previous chapters.

Optional support material for reports

Common sense, appropriateness, or the report requirements dictate whether you use any of the following:
- Letter of transmittal
- Preface or Foreword
- Title page
- Table of contents
- Appendices
- Glossary
- Bibliography
- Index
- Specific format guidelines for an individual business/organization (e.g., the U.S. government has particular format requirements for their documents as do many aerospace-related companies)

Report writing reminders:
- ❑ Always clearly identify your reader
- ❑ Provide adequate background information
- ❑ Establish the scope of the report
- ❑ Collect objective data
- ❑ Form conclusions that arise from data
- ❑ Offer recommendations that arise from conclusions
- ❑ Use headings
- ❑ Present information logically and with a consistent format
- ❑ Edit for readability; proofread for errors
- ❑ Conclude with an abstract or summary

Executive Summary

This stand-alone document is a synopsis of information in a report. A restatement of the most relevant points, it contains enough detail to inform the reader but concise enough to cover the topic's significance.

Though this is usually written last, it is placed before the report's introduction and summarizes the major points (Power 2s) of the report. The **executive summary** can be five sentences or a page but usually no longer. Keep the image of a *one-legged interview*—meaning, equate how long you can stand on one leg to how long you can hold your reader's attention—in the back of your brain. Or use the recommendation from *The Handbook of Technical Writing*, by Brusaw, Alred and Oliu: the summary's length should be no more than 10 percent of the length of the report. Consider bullets and lists to help the reader quickly skim major points.

According to Peggy Jacobson, Ph.D., owner of TCCI, a Seattle-based technical writing and instructional design company, executive summaries differ from company to company, but share some features. Most executive summaries contain four key sections: overview; methods; results and recommendations; and the conclusion. The order of the sections usually mirrors the sequence of the larger report. All executive summaries address readers' needs for clarity about:

- Key problems or concerns
- Specific recommendations or solutions
- Benefits to their business, customers or bottom line

Use the chart below to guide the planning for your next executive summary:

WHO is my reader?	Key question: What do I know about my reader's business and concerns?
WHY was the report written or why did the event take place?	Key question: How can I briefly summarize the purpose of the report?
WHAT main points need to be included in the following areas? • Actions • Results or findings • Recommendations • Benefits	Key question: Which aspects/details are essential to help my reader understand my ideas?
WHEN should recommendations be carried out?	Key question: What timeframe can I suggest? OR What's the best order for implementing the recommendations?
HOW do my recommendations directly benefit my reader?	Key question: Have I anticipated my reader's needs, questions, and concerns?

Once you finish drafting the executive summary, you still have a job to do: revise, revise, revise!

Some final considerations:

Watch your tone:

Executive summaries are concise, but not abrupt or brusque. Remember to picture your reader as you write. You want to sound professional, but not aloof.

Watch your language:

Avoid technical terminology, acronyms, pedantic language, and business jargon. These only distance you from your reader.

Stick to the facts:

An executive summary is not the place for opinions, new references, long explanations, illustrations, or detailed numbers and figures already listed in the report. These only cloud or complicate your presentation.

Here is an example of an executive summary adapted from Dr. Jacobson's technical writing course.

To: Cameron Bourne, SVP
From: Sonja Miller, Human Resources
Date: 3/30/06
Subject: Home Office Procedure Manual project

Overview

The rapid growth of the XYZ Company has resulted in a short-age of written documentation for existing procedures. Within Home Office, under-documented procedures impair commu-nication between departments, resulting in omissions and duplications. The lack of written procedures also lengthens and complicates the learning process for new employees. Improved intra-office communication, project coordination, and train-ing will raise overall cost effectiveness and service quality for the XYZ Company Home Office.

Without documented procedures, the performance of XYZ Company as a whole, and its ability to support its aggres-sive growth, may be compromised.

Since Home Office employees already maintain demanding sched-ules, Business Writing That Counts (BWTC) has been contracted to begin the work of documenting departmental procedures.

Methods

The initial phase of the Procedure Manual project consists of interviews in six Home Office Departments. The first set of interviews was with the leads in:

- *Accounting*
- *Human Resources*
- *Marketing*
- *Management Information Systems*
- *Medical Staffing*
- *Medical Department*

BWTC gathered existing documentation and worked with the interviewees to identify the main procedural topics of their departments. From interview notes and consultation, a detailed outline was developed. The outline structure follows:

I. Management Overview
II. Medical Systems
   A. Medical Organization Overview
   B. Medical Administration Procedures
III. Financial Systems
   A. Financial Systems Organization Overview
   B. Accounting Procedures
   C. Human Resources Procedures
   D. Management Information Systems Procedures
   E. Marketing Procedures
   F. Medical Staffing Procedures

BWTC suggests incorporating figures, screen prints, forms, and tables into the manual.

Results and Recommendations

BWTC estimates, using the 50-page outline as its basis, the finished manual with fully written explanations and illustrations will be from 250-350 pages.

The following issues require discussion:

1. Total scope of project outside initial BWTC proposal
2. Maintenance of the procedure manual updates
3. Separate manual for accounting
4. Decisions about final formatting
5. Decision about final manual: online or print version

Conclusion

This procedure manual will prove invaluable for both new and experienced Home Office employees. The manual, when completed, will directly benefit the company through enhanced intra-office communication and coordination, and will lead to cost-saving efficiencies and improved services to our clients.

Dr. Julie Tip:
You can use the report's table of contents as an organizing guide for your summary.

Proposals

The difference between reports and proposals is found in the actual words themselves. Reports *report* unemotionally about information gathered. They deliver the facts. **Proposals** *propose* and *persuade* a specific course of action, and request action or support from the reader. They attempt to persuade the reader that the product, service or idea presented is the best among many.

Proposals can be a great sales tool. They can persuade or recommend; offer a solution; present a service or product; sell a concept, idea or plan; request or seek permission or approval. The format of your proposal will again depend on its purpose, the circumstances, and the all-important *reader*. Use the specifics of the formal report on the preceding pages as a guide. However, you may want to consider the following elements. This "think sheet" (next page) can give you a start.

On a piece of paper, make four columns labeled *background*, *problem*, *action*, and *plan*. You can also create an Idea Map. Respond to each question and statement below. For example, your company wants to purchase a new software program. Using the sentences below, think about these questions: What information is pertinent? Will the new software solve productivity problems? Who needs what by when? What kind of financial commitment is involved? Who will need training?

From this *Think Sheet*, use the Power Numbers to write your document.

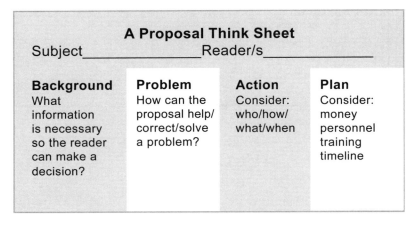

Beginning: Summarize the proposed problem and your plan to solve it. Then address the benefits of your plan. How will your plan help the customer? What benefit does your solution offer your customer? The level of reader knowledge will determine what or how much background information is necessary.

Body: How are your methods, materials, equipment, time, and costs most effective, efficient, and productive? What results can you expect and how will you evaluate them? This can be technical as you describe the plan in detail. A logical approach—one point leading to another— helps the reader. Examples, illustrations, statistics, and/or details help make your case.

Ending: Summarize your key points and reemphasize the benefits. Also, urge the reader to take action and share your willingness to help.

Model Motto: These models are merely guides. Take what you need, ignore the rest.

> **Dr. Julie Tip:**
> If you are writing an RFP (request for proposal) or grant, writing to the specifications is extremely important. Simple as that statement seems, more than half of all submitted proposals are trashed merely because the writers *did not address* the required components.

E-Biz Writing
E-*Everything!*

Everyone is touting the electronic revolution—the speed and the instantaneous of the Internet have caught us up in its velocity. Consider these numbers:

- 97 percent of North American workers rely on e-mail as their main communication tool.
- Some firms estimate top management spends four hours a day just reading e-mails.
- 70,000 blogs are created every day.
- 1.4 trillion e-mails were sent out by American businesses just last year.
- More than 54 million Americans use instant messaging (IM); 11 million use it at work.
- Spam makes up 60 percent of all e-mail.

And one last number: In a recent survey, 80 percent of business professionals stated they would rather do business over the Internet than on the phone. E-mail now seals deals and closes contracts. Writing is alive and well over the Internet—"well" being the operative word, as e-mail, once considered casual conversation, now has recipients *tsk-tsking* at the water cooler over poorly composed messages. And more importantly, senior management now believe if their employees cannot write well, they cannot do the job well either!

An oxymoron

Thanks to e-mail and the Internet, now everyone can communicate quickly and efficiently. Right?

Not necessarily. I challenge this notion that we've finally found the missing link to good communication. In fact, I wonder if the term *e-mail communication* might be an oxymoron. More often than not, we dash off a quick e-mail filled with spelling and punctuation errors we would never allow in a letter. Just because messages move at the speed of light doesn't mean they need to be written at the speed of light.

Cyberspace: the land where grammar and clarity go to die.
~Patricia T. O'Conner

Readers respect and respond to good writing no matter what the medium; therefore, it must become second nature to plan, organize and proof what you've written before you press SEND. Your goal should be 100 percent comprehension by 100 percent of your readers, 100 percent of the time. Read on for some valuable e-mail tips and suggestions that can help you cope. I have organized them around four topics:

- Creating a protocol
- Composing your message
- Considering your medium
- Controlling your time

Creating E-mail Protocol

Oh, the blessing and the curse of the digital revolution! Between e-mail, blogs, instant and text messaging, cell phones, Blackberries and the Internet, we are drowning in data overload. Moreover, constant interruptions caused by our gadgets cost the U. S. economy an estimated $558 billion annually. This staggering number does not add in the cost of poorly written e-mails that land companies and employees in hot legal trouble, destroy long-term client relationships, and ruin reputations—just review Mike Brown's e-mails (former FEMA chief) as Hurricane Katrina raged and you will understand. Add to this mix a lack of civility and common sense and you have an explosive brew.

What to do? For starters, treat e-mail writing as *writing*, not as casual conversation. Whether written in the sky, sent by carrier pigeon or via the Web, words must connect with the reader. Good writing allows this to happen; poor writing does not.

Currently, writing online is still, as author Patricia O'Conner writes, "...in its Wild West stage as a free-for-all with everybody shooting from the hip and no sheriff in sight." Therefore, I would like to establish some law and order by recommending that all companies—from multinationals to sole proprietors—develop an *e-mail protocol*. Simply stated it's "the way we do business around here" in terms of communicating via e-mail with co-workers and customers. It is a code of behavior, a set of standards as to how you will frame your words, manage your inbox, even extend your brand.

Below I've listed key questions to visit at your next meeting. Your answers will shape this company-wide document.

1 **How do you greet and close messages?**
Some companies put together a series of key phrases used solely for openings and closings. Remember, you would never call without greeting someone. Why would you not include a greeting in your e-mails?

2 **What does your e-mail signature say about your company?**
It should be an extension of your company's brand. Professional with no cutesy sayings, it

should contain all contact information. Also, establish a standard for font style and size.

3 **What is the company policy around blind copies?** Some companies only use them for e-blasts; others say they are strictly verboten. Discuss why, when and how you use them.

Where U.S. Online Users Check Their E-mail:

In bed	23%
In the bathroom	4%
While driving	4%
In church	1%

4 **Do you have a message for your Out of Office auto-responder?** How long can you stay away from the office before you turn the responder on? Four hours? One day?

5 **How often do you check e-mails?** Some companies set their programs so e-mails are only called up hourly, thus reducing down time.

6 **How soon do you return e-mails?** Within four hours? By end of business day?

7 **Do you use emoticons?** Buzzing bees, dancing bears, smiley faces. I heartily rule against them.

8 **How many e-mails before you pick up the phone?**

Litigation E-Nightmare Did you see what Dr. XX did today? If that patient survives, it will be a miracle!

The rule of thumb seems to be three. If the issues are not resolved by then, pick up the phone or walk down the hall.

E-mail has become the biggest productivity drain in businesses today, so it's time to bring law and order to the untamed world of your Internet communication. Get a handle on this daily data dump by establishing a protocol—e-mail etiquette, if you will—and you and your company will stand above the crowd.

Composing your message

Every time you make a key stroke, it says something about you. People judge e-mails just like hard copy. In fact, I tell clients to imagine their letterhead stamped on every e-mail they send. I'm not exaggerating when I say that every message represents you *and* your company.

But these cautions shouldn't stop you from writing! In the previous chapters, I gave you tools to compose messages that make an impact and get results. If good writing is good writing no matter what the medium, just apply your new skills to your e-mail messages. Here's how it works.

As a little girl climbed onto Santa's lap, Santa asked the usual, "What would you like for Christmas?" The child stared at him openmouthed and horrified, then gasped, "Didn't you get my e-mail?"

Map your ideas!
Before you touch the key board, grab a piece of paper (gasp!) and jot down your ideas. Don't write out your entire message, just a rough Power framework of key points.

Use those Power Numbers!
Briefly include a Power 1 statement in the subject line of your e-mail. People scan their inboxes. A clear Power 1 will help your reader see the relevance of your message.

See for yourself! Read the subject lines below and consider which one you would look at first:

Version One:

Subject:	Sales Meeting

Subject line leaves too much to the imagination. When? About what?

Version Two:

Subject:	Sales meeting at 2:00 to address new deadlines and product changes

Second version clearly states the meeting's purpose.

List the Power 2s upfront. Consider using bullets for your key points. These help the reader quickly scan. Your reader can then scroll down for the details. Since everyone has a different system for indicating a break in information. I recommend using either the asterisk * or these << >> to draw attention. See the example e-mail message below:

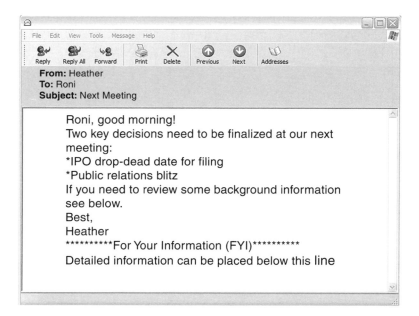

Put your Power 3s, 4s, 5s, in an attachment! Keep your message short and sweet. Include just enough details to make your points clear. Ideally try to make your e-mail fit your computer screen, which calculates to no more than 200-300 words. Few people read past this point. More than one page of information? Attach.

Don't forget Zero Power!
When responding to forwarded messages or issues in an e-mail chain, don't just jump in with a comment. Rather, include enough background or context about prior discussions to make your comments clear to all readers. For example, imagine reading this message:

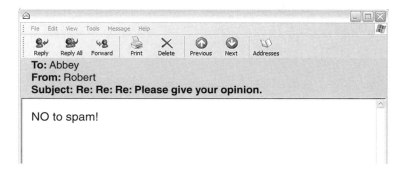

Is Robert talking about the lunch special? An old problem with a slowing business? A new marketing strategy? If you haven't been in the e-mail loop, you will need to back up three messages to understand his response.

Before you answer a question or send a comment to the group, decide whether you need to include a brief introduction to help all readers understand the issue and your response. A little context goes a long way:

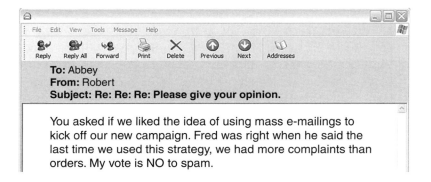

To: Abbey
From: Robert
Subject: Re: Re: Re: Please give your opinion.

You asked if we liked the idea of using mass e-mailings to kick off our new campaign. Fred was right when he said the last time we used this strategy, we had more complaints than orders. My vote is NO to spam.

Remember—Zero Power works at the end of your message, too. You can build rapport with a sentence or two that lets readers know you value their business or their feedback.

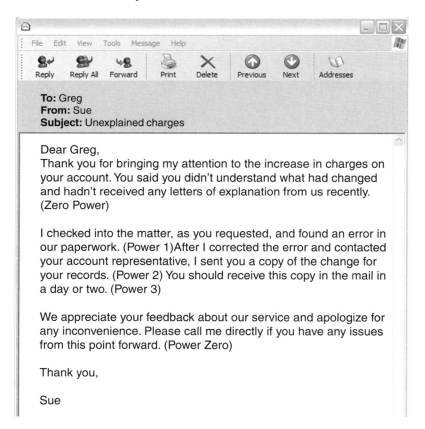

To: Greg
From: Sue
Subject: Unexplained charges

Dear Greg,
Thank you for bringing my attention to the increase in charges on your account. You said you didn't understand what had changed and hadn't received any letters of explanation from us recently. (Zero Power)

I checked into the matter, as you requested, and found an error in our paperwork. (Power 1)After I corrected the error and contacted your account representative, I sent you a copy of the change for your records. (Power 2) You should receive this copy in the mail in a day or two. (Power 3)

We appreciate your feedback about our service and apologize for any inconvenience. Please call me directly if you have any issues from this point forward. (Power Zero)

Thank you,

Sue

Notice in the e-mail above the writer told the reader what to do next. Need a reply? Using the acronym *RSVP* is a shortcut that can also guide your recipient's actions. Need co-workers to make decisions? Some professionals prefer to type the words *Action Required* and list the activities needing attention. This list can even come *before* the body of the text. Check your company's protocol!

Don't forget to be C.L.E.V.R.! (see Chapter Four)

Proofread, proofread, and proofread. NO excuses. Whether you put pen to paper or fingers to the keyboard, three read-throughs is still your mantra. In fact, really important e-mails should be printed out and read as hard copy.

Let's review a few revision tips that will help you add professional polish to your e-mails:

- Keep your words, sentences and paragraphs short. Follow the twenty-one rule.
- Avoid passive voice. Say NO! to *to-be* verbs.
- Use transitions to help the reader follow your logic.
- Avoid jargon, acronyms, pedantic and biased language.
- Make messages easy on the eye. Use bullets, white space, bolding, headers to aid understanding.
- Proofread out loud and use spell-check.

Considering Your Medium

Though the ease and convenience of e-mail can be appealing, cultural mores may dictate otherwise. For example, in some countries, it is considered very bad form to have an electronic communiqué be the first point of contact with a client. As we increase our global networks, pay closer attention to cultural differences and how your message may be interpreted.

Always determine the best medium for your message. Remember your reader! Remember your purpose! If e-mail works, a few DOs and DON'Ts may keep you out of trouble.

E-mail DOs
- Do think through your message.
- Do beware of the *forward* feature: keep the original sender out of trouble. Edit content until appropriate for the intended recipient.
- Double-check the "To" field to make sure you're sending the message to the right person.
- Do use a positive tone—remember that you are representing your organization with each e-mail you send.
- Do mind your manners. *Please* and *thank you* have not gone out of style.
- Decide how long you want to be stuck in an e-mail chain before you pick up the phone.
- Check your tone—be careful with humor, sarcasm, exaggeration and speculation because you could be misunderstood and text out of context is hard to explain.

E-mail DON'Ts
- No SHOUTING or whispering.
- Don't put anything in an e-mail you wouldn't put in a memo or say to your mother.
- Don't catch (or send) a virus! Never open an attachment unless you have scanned for a virus.
- Don't send mass mailings, broadcast messages or jokes without manager approval.
- Don't respond to a flamed message.
- Don't send raw data or large attachments.
- Don't send *BCCs*.
- Don't include cutesy sayings or whimsical words of wisdom in your signature file.
- Don't use e-mail to deliver bad news. A phone call or face-to-face talk may be better.

- Don't send confidential information—Again: say it in person.
- Don't send anything that could be considered discriminatory, harassing or break the law.

Controlling Your Time

We've taken care of the customer. We've taken care of your company. Now it's time to take care of you. I bet you now receive ten times more e-mail messages than snail mail. Manage your e-mails as you would other correspondences that cross your desk: *Handle it only once!*

Here's how:

Litigation E-Nightmare
Yes, I know we shipped 100 barrels of _____, but on our end, steps have been taken to ensure no record exists. If you know what I mean.

1   **Promise yourself to check e-mail twice daily.** Time management of your e-mails remains crucial for sanity. Checking in twice a day allows you to handle your messages in a timely and professional manner without being chained to your computer. E-mail messages, like phone messages, should be returned within twenty-four hours.

2   **Manage your e-mail.** As you scan your e-mail, decide whether you will
   - Delegate: Not your area of expertise? Forward it on!
   - Delete: Older than three months? It's history...or at least material for a reference file.
   - Do it: Rule of thumb: if it will take less than two minutes, respond.
   - Defer: Assign a date and time to respond later. Use Outlook to set this up.

3 Create a folder per project; create files with the same names.
Time management demands you control the onslaught. Organize data into files and folders, then prioritize folders according to the project you're working on or the message frequency from one client. For project management, an

Sloppy e-mail gets the tongues wagging about the writer's literal failings.
-Complete Idiot's Guide to Office Politics

efficient system is mandatory. Also, on important e-mails, consider cc'ing yourself so your files will contain complete sets of key correspondences.

4 Answer briefly—others will learn to expect it.
Get in the habit of writing concise, to-the-point messages but with a personal touch. You'll quickly teach others not to expect a long, detailed answer from you. Wayne McKinnon gives this tip in his book, *The Complete Guide to E-Mail*: For a brief response, just writing in the subject line may be enough. You can insert the letters EOM (end of message) followed by brackets.

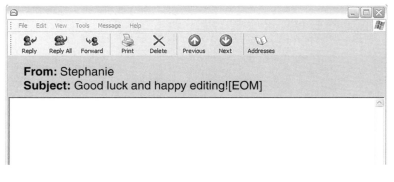

5 Turn on an *Out of Office* responder in your absence.
Courtesy counts!

! *Don't multitask while you're reading your e-mail. You* *end up having to reread because of your lack of concentration, and thereby waste valuable time.*

6 **Consider using this checklist to remind your-** **self about what's important.**

Questions to ask before hitting SEND

Accuracy
- √ Are all spelling, punctuation, and usage mistakes eliminated?
- √ Are your facts correct?
- √ Have you double-checked included dates, days, and times?
- √ Are all promised documents attached?

Relevance
- √ Is the content of your message business-related?
- √ Is the e-mail appropriate to send to everyone on your list?
- √ Have you met all confidentiality requirements?
- √ Does your tone match the subject and your audience?
- √ Is the subject line appropriate for your e-mail's content?
- √ Does any part of your message seem emotionally charged or insulting?
- √ Have you included everything your audience needs to know?
- √ Does your e-mail follow a logical progression?
- √ Is your e-mail too long or too short?
- √ Is your material timely?
- √ How do you feel when you read your e-mail?
- √ Do all recipients know what they are supposed to do in response to your e-mail?

BLOGS

I can't let this section close without briefly touching on blogs. A blog is a contraction of the words *Web log* and is used as either a noun (a blog) or a verb (blogging). *Wikipedia,* the free online encyclopedia, defines it as a Web site where items are posted regularly and displayed in reverse chronological order. Blogs often focus on a particular subject, such as food, politics, or local news. Some blogs function as online diaries. A typical blog combines text, images and links to other blogs, Web pages, and other media related to its topic. Since its appearance in 1995, blogging has emerged as a popular means of communication, affecting public opinion and mass media around the world.

Journalists, hobbyists, scientists, educators, CEOs and techies are just some of the groups that use them to share personal stories and opinions, comments on the news, recent discoveries and links with friends and families. Companies use B-Blogs (business blogs) as part of their marketing strategy. They view them as vehicles to connect with their customers in a more personal way. Often written in first person, blogs allow readers to become engaged in a topic, respond to it and build a relationship with the writer and the company.

The jury is still out on this new electronic communication tool. According to Elizabeth Osder, bloggers are "navel-gazers." "And they're about as interesting as friends who make you look at their scrap books." She added, "There's an over fascination here with self-expression, with opinion. This is opinion without expertise, without resources, without reporting." We still don't know the impact of blogs. Though recently, some bloggers have been fired and sued for their postings. A word of caution: use your words carefully!

Some tips if you choose to blog :

* Use a genuinely engaging voice
* Keep a conversational tone
* Remember grammar, punctuation, and spelling still count
* Focus on clarity as your goal
* Use anecdotes and stories
* Keep the topic narrow
* Be clear on who your target audience is
* Use humor where appropriate

Fax Facts

Here's a short list of tips for faxing.

1 **Cover sheets are important pieces of paper.** Be sure they have the following information: sender's name, company, address, phone number, and fax and e-mail address. Always indicate how many pages are being sent. It's a courtesy as well as a precaution.

Another Wayne McKinnon Tip: Ask recipients if they require a cover sheet. Home-office recipients often don't want or need one. Sticky notes can be purchased that are specifically designed for faxing.

2 **Cover sheets are also the first image that your customer has of you.** When you compose your cover sheet, let professionalism guide your design.

3 **Don't send any correspondence in smaller than 10-point font or written with colored ink.** It won't transmit well.

4 If you have documents with pictures that you send frequently, have a low-resolution copy on hand for faxing. Most high-resolution pictures appear as an all-black object. 150 dots per inch (DPI) may work well. Low-resolution, high-contrast images work best.

5 Sending faxed documents directly from your computer produces a better quality document than one sent via a low-resolution fax machine.

6 When designing a cover fax sheet, fax to yourself for review.

All Write, Already!

We've entered a new millennium and tougher, leaner times. Tougher to get business. Tougher to keep business. Customers demand more, yet must operate with slimmer budgets; companies function with fewer employees who shoulder more responsibilities. This current business environment demands maximizing efficiency and reducing waste. Getting to the meat of the issue in writing is even more important than ever. Time is king. We are all watching it, reducing it, saving it—from the manufacturing floor to the boardroom.

The business-writing strategies in this book will assist you in reducing your writing time and increasing your productivity. Through thousands of workshops and the cumulative training of over a million professionals, we've learned what counts and what doesn't when it comes to business writing. Whether writing is a core competency or something you have to do as part of your job, using these cost-effective writing tools will save you and your company time and money. And, you can take that to the bank!

I leave you with a final checklist.

The Last Ever Writer's Checklist

Did you...

√   Idea Map the topic? (Chapter One)

√   Use the Power Numbers to build your document? (Chapter Two and Three)

√   Draft the document by free-writing with an edge? (Chapter Two)

√   Write like you talk? (Chapter Three)

√   Employ Zero Power sentences where appropriate? (Chapter Three)

√   Consider tricky transitions a new strategy for your writer's tool box? (Chapter Three)

√   Practice the C.L.E.V.R. solutions to business writing? (Chapter Four)

√   Solicit feedback for your writing? (Chapter Four)

√   Use correct punctuation, capitalization, and spelling? (Chapter Five)

√   Avoid disaster before your message went out? (Chapter Five)

√   Understand the protocol to electronic communications? (Chapter Six)

√   Learn the basic formats of day-to-day business writing? (Chapter Six)

√   Have fun? (Chapters One to Six)

Congratulations! By working through these six chapters, you've acquired a complete set of tools for writing quickly and effectively. You are ready to write documents that get read!

But wait—don't close the book just yet. This fourth edition of *Business Writing That Counts!* offers something extra—a special bonus section that will show you how to take your sales writing to a higher level. So, if you'd like to use your newfound writing skills to improve your sales, just turn the page.

BUSINESS

WRITING THAT

SELLS!

Jonathan Todd

Introduction to

Business Writing That Sells!

D o you want your sales writing to get results every time?

Then you're in luck.

I have asked Jonathan Todd, internationally recognized sales and marketing expert, to offer additional value to my readers by giving the *real scoop* on sales writing. In the following special section, *Business Writing That Sells!*, Jonathan shares invaluable techniques on how to turn any sales document into a selling machine.

In reading *Business Writing That Sells!*, you will be attending a virtual sales seminar presented by one of the country's most prolific marketers. Jonathan first explains the theory behind his distinctive methodology, then guides you through its practical application using exercises and models. By the time you reach the end of this thoroughly entertaining and educational sales writing course, you will not only know what sells and why, you will be able to put it into words.

Yeah, yeah, I know you marketing pros out there think it's the same old, same old. Not so! Give this section a thorough read whether you've been in the business for only a short time or since forever. Jonathan's approach is fresh, innovative, and results-oriented—and he's got a long list of successful and high-profile clients to prove it. So don't miss this opportunity to learn from one of the best. You will come away knowing *how to sell the write way!*

BUSINESS WRITING THAT SELLS!

Learning to Sell the Write Way!

The pen is mightier than the sword. You're about to become armed and dangerous, using only the written word.

You've already seen how quickly and effectively you can write using the Power Numbers system. In this section, I'm going to show you how to take your newfound writing prowess and use it to sell, and sell well.

It doesn't matter if you're already a sales pro or if the very thought of selling causes beads of sweat to pop onto your brow. Read and work through this special sales section and you will notice some exciting changes. Your income will likely increase, you'll be offered job promotions, you will gain new clients—in general, you will get a rocket-blast forward in whatever

Selling (1) a : to develop a belief in the truth, value, or desirability of : gain acceptance for <trying to sell a program to the Congress> b : to persuade or influence to a course of action or to the acceptance of something <sell children on reading>
-Excerpted from the Merriam-Webster Dictionary

you're doing. Your peers will envy you, and you'll never have to do the dishes at home again. (Okay, you might still have to do the dishes.) But, commit a few hours to this section, and you will definitely learn how to sell in an easy, comfortable, honest, cool way.

Why Sell Through Writing

This section on sales and marketing writing is a radical addition to the third edition of *Business Writing That Counts*. Radical but necessary. Necessary because the world is moving faster.

Writing began as an extension of the gesture and spoken word, a more sophisticated way to get one's point across to others. In today's world, we've taken the concept a step further: We don't want to just communicate our point, but to persuade others to agree with us. I call that "power-selling."

Think about it. No matter what you write, you're trying to sell the reader.

- As a tradesperson, you write sales copy to convince the reader to buy your product.
- As a manager, you write a memo to garner support and get the gang on board.
- As a CFO, you write your annual report to show your stockholders they've invested well.
- As a service provider, you write an RFP that explains why you deserve the contract.
- As an irate customer, you write your complaint letter to get action and resolve your problem.

It's not just enough to write good sales copy, however. Thanks to e-mail and other advances in technology, you not only need to know how to write persuasively, but how to do it quickly. Anything you write needs to hit home fast and accomplish your goal—NOW. But that's okay, because you're about to get tools you need to sell better and faster. Say, "Hallelujah!"

Business Writing Versus Sales Writing

In the first six chapters of this book you learned from one of the nation's top business-writing gurus how to transform your writing in a matter of hours. By following Dr. Miller's system, you became skilled at *business* writing. In this section, you will enhance those skills by learning *sales* writing.

There is an important difference between business writing and sales writing. I look at it this way:

In business writing, your goal is to communicate information to your reader.

In sales writing your goal is to guide your reader toward taking a desired action.

Being able to make the distinction between these two types of writing will give you a tremendous edge when it comes to marketing and sales. In short, you will be able to power-sell.

Sales writing can be broken down into two categories:

1. **The selling of a product or service.**
2. **The selling of an idea or the writer's position.**

Each of these two types of sales writing can lead to some kind of financial payment or other tangible compensation. The second one may also have as its goal a shift in the reader's position on a subject the writer is "selling."

However, in both cases, the theory and methodology for sales writing is the same—to lead the reader to take a desired action. And to do that, you must understand how your words affect your reader.

In the following pages, you will learn the **psychology** of how **opinion** is molded by words into **motivation** for the reader; how motivation is **directed** to **persuade** the reader to take the **action** you want; and how that action is taken within a **specified timeframe**.

As you can see, by the time you reach the end of this section you will indeed be armed and dangerous.

The cave

Follow me back in time, some 450,000 years ago, to a small cave in what is now southern France. Cold and hungry, Ulla huddles near her man, Muk, who is deep asleep. Both are wrapped in layers of furs, as they have not yet mastered fire. The bow and arrow will not be invented for another 430,000 years. Alphabets and writing tools will not appear on the scene for another 444,000 years, give or take a hundred centuries. Life is primitive.

Ulla pokes at Muk with a stick until he wakes up. She points to her stomach, opens her mouth to indicate hunger, and makes a growling noise. Using the stick, she draws the shape of a small animal on the cave's dirt floor. Muk

While Ulla and Muk are fictional, the timelime, town, and historical data presented here are true and based on current research and theories.

shakes his head to signify, "no" and settles down to go back to sleep. Ulla pokes Muk again and shows him a small hand tool she had crafted earlier in the day. She offers it to Muk who smiles, takes the tool, and prepares to go out into the cold to hunt for food.

Having drawn the animal in the dirt and handed Muk the tool, Ulla has written one of history's first sales letters—and closed the sale.

The Ulla and Muk in all of us compresses the concept of selling into an "I want—you give me" paradigm. While this is remedial selling, it is still basic sales, and we'll talk more about refining this concept later in this section. The point here is that if Ulla could sell 450,000 years ago, so can you. In fact, you already do sell pretty well. You just need to unlock your power-selling potential.

A genetically honed selling machine

Selling comes naturally, instinctively to each of us. Sales ability is in our genetic memory, literally practiced by every ancestor we've ever had, going further back than Ulla and Muk. Mankind's internal selling skills are right up there with the drive to survive. Our ancestors necessarily were good salespeople; if they hadn't been, they would have perished, and then where would we be? Crude, cruel but true.

All of us are selling all the time. We have wants and needs that are often at odds with those around us. We sell at home to get Chinese food instead of Mexican food for dinner. We sell through interviews to get jobs. We sell at work to enhance our internal corporate value or to further the company goals.

So if we're so good at it, why is selling, and thus sales writing, so difficult for so many? Why do most people have a fear and hatred of selling, including those salespeople who claim they "love" to sell?

Why most people hate selling and sales writing

Take a moment and write down three reasons that make selling difficult for you:

1. _____

2. _____

3. _____

Most people don't like sales, salespeople, or sales writing because the traditional notion of sales is adversarial, confrontational, argumentative, and pushy. It evokes a distasteful win or lose, me or you, black or white feeling.

The "I want—you give me" paradigm suggested by the Ulla and Muk scenario promotes a sales concept used by poorly trained sales people. It's based on a numbers game, where if the seller pushes enough people regularly, some will cave in and do his bidding.

To put it another way, selling used to be based on imposing the seller's ideas onto others. Not any more!

The New Sales Theory

Guided teamwork: moving from win-lose to win-win

Okay, we all agree that the win-lose model is distasteful at best and downright debilitating for most of us. So, let's take a look at sales in another light—within the newer concept of win-win.

Positioning selling in a business environment as a win-win proposition is now a necessity and can best be accomplished through *guided teamwork*.

Guided teamwork leads to mutually beneficial results. The salesperson acts as the conductor of the team—which consists of both the sellers and the buyers—with the common goal being both sides getting what they want. Even if the salesperson is operating solo and attempting to sell a thing or concept to a single buyer, the salesperson must position herself as the team leader of both seller and buyer. In more complex organizational sales, the salesperson must take the role of bringing the sales teams and allied departments together with the buying teams and their involved departments to facilitate a win-win.

If you view and act upon the sales writing process as a facilitator bringing mutual benefits to people with diverse agendas, the process is pleasant. You make friends, solve problems together, with each person benefiting from your efforts. It also humanizes the selling process which takes the rejection, fear, and loathing out of sales writing.

Now that we have a working theory, let's look at the concepts, psychology, and components of *sales writing*. We'll take a top down approach beginning with the goal and moving to the mechanisms that support the big picture of excellence in *sales writing*.

Writing to Power-Sell

In the twenty-first century, effective sales writing can no longer rely on the direct, one-sided persuasive approach. If you want to improve your sales writing and move up to power-selling, you must guide the reader, so that he concludes for himself that the value of what you are offering is greater than the cost. When the reader does so, he then automatically shifts to take the desired action—the action that both you and he now want.

Power-selling definition: Effectively guiding the reader to come to his own conclusion that the *value*, i.e., the units of reader benefit, is worth more than the *cost*, i.e., the units of reader detriment, so that he takes the desired action within the writer's specified timeframe.

This concept becomes the standard by which you test all your sales writing.

Sales Writing Tip:
You want to guide your reader so he decides that the benefit of what you're offering outweighs the cost. Based on that, the reader decides to take (or move closer to) your recommended action.

We'll discuss this in depth as we move through this section and you learn how to write to power-sell. The following quiz will get you started down the path to understanding this important concept.

Practice: Sales writing practice #1

Read the power-selling definition above a couple of times thinking carefully about what makes a good sale. Once you understand the definition, take a look at the following example of a good sales letter. Match the letter's sentences to the power-selling definition:

Letter #1

Dear Mr. Smith,

You already have our full, written proposal to redo your current Web site, so we just wanted to send you a quick follow-up. The proposal I sent you last week offers to replace your current Web site with a new ACME-WEB site which upgrades your graphics and enhances your marketing message.

We're the best Web design firm available for the lowest prices in this area. We have more designers than our competition, more awards, and more happy customers. All components for review are available for your approval online as we create them.

Contracting with our company within 30 days provides you with a 10 percent discount ($5,000 off our $50,000 package). Your new Web site can be operational 20 days from your work-order.

Based on your Web counter statistics of an average 7,900 hits a day, we think it makes sense to act quickly. We can get started right now with phone and fax authorization. You can reach me at (555) 555-5555. We can discuss any questions you may have and then get started on the project.

Looking forward to working together!

Regards,

Jim
ACME-WEB

Now you try it

Use the following checklist to verify that this letter meets the criteria set forth for power-selling writing as defined above:

❑ Does the reader understand the "benefits"?
❑ Does the reader understand the "costs"?

❑ Does the reader conclude that "benefits" outweigh "costs"?

❑ Does the reader choose to act within the
timeframe?

Does the reader understand the benefits?

The benefits offered in the letter appear to be:
- Upgraded graphics
- Enhanced image
- Best Web design
- Lowest prices in the area
- Most designers
- More awards
- More happy customers
- $5,000 off if action taken within 30 days

While this all sounds pretty good, most of what the
writer discusses in this letter falls under the category of
"features" not "benefits."

So, the answer to is NO! The writer only THINKS the
reader understands the benefits.

Sales Writing Tip:
When writing to sell, always makes sure products
and services are explained in terms of the *benefits*
they bring to the reader.

As you may have guessed by now, while I set up this
example as a good sales letter, it isn't a GREAT sales letter.
It does illustrate some of the traps writers can fall into,
such as viewing puffing, features, and slick wording
as benefits.

Let's explore the rest of the test questions.

2 *Does the reader understand the costs?*

Most people check YES because the $50,000 price is listed. Again, the answer is NO.

The reader understands the *price*, but we defined the *cost* to the reader in terms of *units of reader detriment*. That's more than the price.

Units of reader detriment include not only the monetary cost, but any other tradeoffs or concessions the reader will be making.

In this example the "money" is $50,000, but the real "cost" (each a unique unit of detriment) includes the concerns the reader may have such as: downtime for changing from the current site to a new site, fear that the writer's firm may not be able to accomplish the task to the reader's satisfaction, resistance to change itself, and the extra cash needed to host a bigger site each month.

Sales Writing Tip:
When writing any sales letter or sales copy that includes the price, be sure to clarify specific benefits the reader will gain that outweigh any perceived units of reader detriment.

3 *Does the reader conclude the benefits outweigh the costs?*

The answer is NO. Nothing in the letter indicates the reader would come to this determination on her own.

To ensure that the reader understands that the benefits outweigh costs, the content in the letter needs to address both sides of this equation. Simply outlining the features won't do that; the writer must show how those features lead to benefits that give more value than the overall cost.

If you don't guide the reader toward the benefits you offer, she will filter your words through her own values, weighing the units of detriment and benefits through her perception to determine how to proceed. Your job in writing to sell is to describe the benefit units so well that she can't help but see their value as you do.

The difficulty faced in this letter is that a tangible (price/detriment) is weighed against an intangible (the merit of a new Web site/benefit). The tangible cost is easy to assess; the intangible benefits are not. In this letter, the writer failed to give tangible weight to the intangible benefits.

4 *Does the reader choose to act within the timeframe?*

The answer to this last question is, again, probably NO, although this aspect is highly subjective and more difficult to measure.

Although the writer extends an offer to discount the service by 10 percent if the reader acts within a certain time limit, more than likely that won't be enough to tip the scales to the benefits side by itself.

Unfortunately, in this example, the writer doesn't make any statement that helps the reader weigh the costs against the benefits; the reader is not directed to discover the benefits outweigh the costs. In sales writing it is essential for the reader to make this a personal choice.

Helping the reader to choose to act is not "the close." Closing is an antiquated set of techniques performed by a seller to manipulate a buyer. It is far more elegant and honorable to allow the buyer to come to his own conclusion that the benefits outweigh the costs. Once the scale tips in favor of the benefits, acting on the offer becomes nearly automatic for most readers/buyers.

> Sales Writing Tip:
> Always approach sales writing with the objective of allowing the readers to "close" themselves.

The four points of power-selling

Power-selling is built on a foundation anchored by four essential cornerstones: benefits, costs, weight, and tracking.

- **Benefits** - what the reader will gain
- **Costs** - what the reader must give up, both monetarily and through other concessions
- **Weight** - comparing the costs against the benefits
- **Tracking** - guiding the reader to make his own conclusion to act within your time parameters

If you want your writing to power-sell, make sure you include all four points in your sales documents.

Rewriting with power selling points in mind

I've rewritten the sample letter to incorporate the four essential points in writing to power-sell. As you read through the letter, I've noted where either benefits, costs, weight, or tracking has been used by the writer.

✎ Practice: Sales writing practice #2

LETTER #2

Dear Mr. Smith,

By the time you've read this short letter, 11 potential buyers will have browsed over to your current Web site, based on your Web counter statistics of an average 7,900 hits a day. The pro- — benefits
posal I sent you last week offers to replace your current Web site with a new ACME-WEB site, which upgrades your graphics and enhances your marketing message by revising copy and modernizing the look, feel and navigation of your site. If your site was up today, these 11 buyers — benefits
would have a greater trust of BIG-CORP, a deeper understanding of BIG-CORP's offerings, and an enhanced likelihood of purchasing BIG-CORP services.

costs

Your new Web site can be operational 20 days — benefits
from your order to begin work. In fact, we'll replace your home page within two days so you receive a near instantaneous image improvement for visitors. We're the best Web design firm avail- costs
able for the lowest prices in this area, based on our trends survey (attached in our proposal). We have more designers than our competition, more — benefits
awards and more happy customers. This means we're more likely to satisfy your artistic and business needs than any other firm you could con- — weight
sider. Our customer satisfaction program ensures you'll be satisfied with our work or we'll continue to make changes (per contract terms) without

costs until you have the BIG-CORP site you determine is right for you.

With the number of site visitors you have, coupled _____ weight
*with your current closure rates, we believe the
changes proposed will literally pay for themselves
within three months.*

*During your lunch hour today, 330 prospects will
see the current site, which you've told me is un-
representative of BIG-CORP. We can change this
without down time and with limited impact to* ⟋ weight
*your schedule as all components for review are
available for your approval on-line as we create
them. While we have 30 days left on our 10% off* ⟋ tracking
*certificate, each day we wait means 7,900
potential customers see the current site. That's* ⟋ tracking
*7,900 people getting the wrong image of BIG-
CORP plus the probability of lost sales.*

Mr. Smith, I promise to make the transition pain- ⟋ tracking
less for you. We can get started right now with _____ costs
*phone and fax authorization. You can reach me
at (555) 555-5555. We can discuss any ques-* ⟋ weight
*tions you may have and begin enhancing your
electronic image and on-line sales instantly. Your* _____ tracking
*7,900 daily visitors don't walk into your office
each day, but they are in your "virtual world"
We're ready to help you serve them.*

Looking forward to working together!

Regards,

*Jim
ACME-WEB*

Now you try it

Take out a recent proposal, e-mail, letter, brochure, commercial, advertisement, or other sales or marketing document. As you read through it, indicate which of the four power-selling points—benefits, costs, weight, or tracking—each sentence primarily reflects. For Zero Power sentences and sentences that don't primarily support one of the four points, simply write "none."

If you don't find at least one of each power-selling point, your document is unlikely to be a good sales piece. Try adding a sentence or two for each missing power-selling point and see if it isn't more persuasive and mutually beneficial.

Finally, go through the document again—but this time read only those sentences marked with benefits, costs, weight, and tracking. Read it out loud from the beginning to the end, skipping any sentence that doesn't represent one of the four points. You should recognize a clean, clear message that provides all the components your reader needs to accept your offer.

Sales Writing Tip:
Before you send any sales letter, test it for the four Power-Selling Points while it's still in draft form. If you don't clearly see the benefits, costs, weight, and tracking, rewrite until you do!

Welcome to Never, Neverland

The delightful story of Peter Pan is centered on Neverland. Although alluring, Neverland doesn't exist—not for grownups! While Neverland tugs at our hearts we can't go there—not anymore.

There are places we'd like to go in sales writing, based on that old Ulla and Muk in each of us, that we no longer can visit. Let's explore some of the Neverlands you'll never be using again in power-selling.

1 It's never *just* about the *price!*

At least once a week in my consulting practice I hear someone say he lost a deal because someone beat his price. Price is *never* the sole factor in making or breaking a deal. If it were, there would be no sales reps, no marketing teams, no people selling anything, anywhere. All we'd need to help us decide what to buy is the giant super-computer price-sorter. Everyone would jump on the Internet, seek the lowest price, and buy.

In the Real World:

A school district put out a request for proposal (RFP) for millions of sheets of blank paper. Stacey and Mark, competing paper brokers, each replied with a proposal. While they both offered exactly the same paper from the same manufacturer, and Stacey's cost was 6% higher than Mark's, Stacey won the contract. When Mark asked why, the purchaser replied, "Stacey offered to deliver paper whenever we ran out. Good prices don't do us any good if we have to go without until our next scheduled delivery."

It doesn't work this way and never will. Even at those Web sites, like eBay and Priceline.com, where similar or the same items are ranked by price, buyers don't blindly choose the lowest figure. Many other factors come into play. Is the seller trustworthy? What's the warranty? How do shipping, handling, insurance, and tax play into the equation? How does the buyer *feel* about the seller?

Even commodities aren't judged wholly on price. Brands have perceived values. Consider the following:

- Have you ever passed on the local market's less expensive private label beef and barley soup, even though the ingredients and serving size were identical to Progresso's?
- Are you ready to outfit that family SUV with 4-ply radial tires made by CHEAP-EX? Or would you feel more comfortable if your daughter rode to school in the snow on NAME-BRAND 4-ply-radials? Isn't a radial 4-ply tire a radial with 4-ply? What's the difference?
- Do you buy any old insurance, based on the lowest price? Or do you respond to the advertising, the agent, or the company?

The answer in all of these is, of course, that you perceive a higher quality in the name you know or in a person you can connect with, even if the items or services appear to be identical.

Sales Writing Tip:
Never base your sales writing on price alone. Even if price appears to be the only issue, dig into the benefits only you can offer, and you'll find price to be negotiable.

2 It's Never about *features*. It's Always about *benefits!*

While this concept may be completely new for some of you, I know you veteran salespeople out there already know a feature from a benefit. Hang on—this discussion gets pretty advanced and will likely deepen your understanding and use of "benefit statements."

Let's first define the difference between these two terms:

Features are the specific **attributes** of an item or concept.
Benefits are the **advantages** features provide.

To guide this discussion, we'll use examples of features and benefits for a product. The same principles hold true for services, but are sometimes a bit harder to recognize. Master the products and the services will come easily.

Here's an advertising statement made up exclusively of features:

The EverFlowing line of fountain pens offer pure silver barrels with 24K gold nibs and broad points.

It sounds good, but lacks the power of real benefits to help the reader weigh the true cost. The features are **pure silver barrels**, **24K gold nibs,** and **broad points**.

Practice: Sales writing practice #3

Staying just on the pen features discussed so far, write down some benefits of these features. You can add to the table I've provided below or use the Idea Map I've created for you. I've started you out with some ideas. On the Idea Map, benefits are shown in gray tone.

Benefit Table

Feature	Benefit
Silver Barrel	Heft, balance, rich feeling, _____, _____, _____
Gold Nib	Shapes to user, _____, _____, _____
Broad Point	Smooth writing experience, Luxuriant writing experience, _____, _____

Figure 1

Idea Map

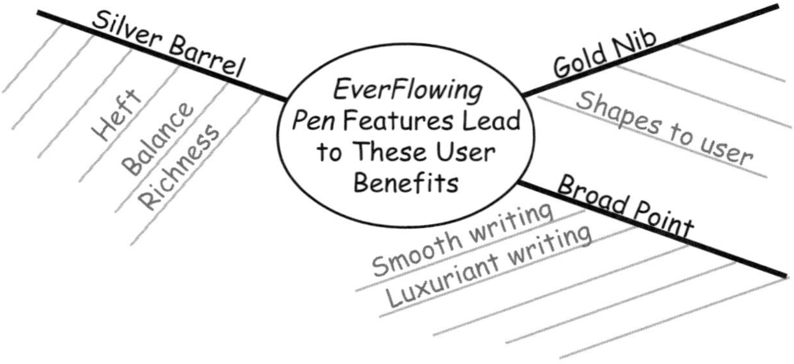

EverFlowing Pen Features Lead to These User Benefits

Silver Barrel — Heft, Balance, Richness

Gold Nib — Shapes to user

Broad Point — Smooth writing, Luxuriant writing

Figure 2

You can use the same Idea Maps you worked with in your business writing to regularly uncover features and benefits as shown in this example. Try making a features/benefit map for one of your own sales letters.

Generally, benefits bring recognizable value to what the features do or illustrate why the features were selected.

I've rewritten the ad copy to use the features of the pen to sell benefits. Take a look at how the copy helps guide the reader to understand the benefits, showing why the features have meaning and value to the reader.

EverFlowing fountain pens feature silver barrels providing heft, balance, and a rich feeling. Our gold nibs and broad points bend and shape themselves to the owner's individual style and pressure, for a smooth and luxuriant writing experience.

How far you want to go with the features is up to you. How you choose to frame the features depends on the type of writing you're doing and who your audience is. More about writing to your audience later.

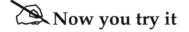 **Now you try it**

I've rewritten the ad copy again using many more benefits. See if you can identify just the benefits by highlighting or underlining each benefit in the copy below:

In the Real World:

Addressing your audience is important. Ad lore has it that when the Scandinavian vacuum manufacturer Electrolux offered its product in America, they chose the slogan: "Nothing sucks like an Electrolux."

The EverFlowing line of fountain pens offers pure silver barrels, with 24K gold nibs and broad points. Unlike today's trend toward disposable, inexpensive, plastic writing tools, the EverFlowing line offers a serious, heavier, satisfying feeling.

European hand-craftsmanship renders each pen a unique masterpiece. Only 24K gold is used for our nibs, as the gold's softness allows the nib to bend and conform to each user's writing style – and soon become an "old friend." Our broad points are the hallmark of an EverFlowing pen, providing commanding boldness and satisfying flow to every stroke, every word, every thought. The simple act of removing the cap and exposing the glistening point, or seating the cap on the barrel end with a distinctive snap, reminds the owner he or she is important, privileged, and certainly worthy of the finer things in life. To hold an EverFlowing pen is to instantly experience the anticipation of the great writing which simply must issue forth from a writing instrument of this caliber.

(Check your answers against those at the back of this section.)

Now that you have a solid grounding in features and benefits and know without a doubt that **it's always about benefits...**

...I need to tell you that **benefits alone are meaningless!**

Here's the next Neverland rule:

Ad lore has it:

The Chevrolet Nova was introduced to Mexico in 1972. General Motors did not take into account that "Nova" is close to "no va"—which in Spanish literally means "doesn't go."

3 **It's never about the *benefits themselves.* It's always about *how* the *reader perceives* the benefits!**

The latest version of ad copy for the EverFlowing pen has limited ability to move some people, because consideration was given only to benefits, *not* to the various classes of readers. Here are some groups or target markets that would likely not respond:

- Left-handed writers would wonder if all that nib bending worked for them.

- Parents would be unlikely to buy this pen for their school-aged children.
- People with jewelry allergies, especially to silver, are out.
- People who are frugal, "practical," or living on fixed incomes would see buying this pen as frivolous.

If you want to address these target markets, new benefits need to be explained. Since these are all relatively small or vertical niche markets, you may not want to address them, or you may choose to create different copy for specific uses targeting these niche markets, such as for inclusion in a left-handed catalog.

Practice: Sales writing practice #4

List three other groups who are being ignored by the EverFlowing pen ad. The more you think about different groups and how they'll respond (or won't respond), the better armed you'll be to offer benefits.

1. _____

2. _____

3. _____

In my marketing practice, my team at SabreMark, Inc., can almost always increase current sales of a product or service just by reviewing the marketing and sales copy, Web site, and communications, and then extending the **benefit statement** to encompass more markets.

Let's take a look at how one of the markets left out of the EverFlowing pen example—parents buying the product for their children—could be addressed. One way to target that market is shown with the following benefit statement:

The gift of an EverFlowing pen to school-aged children teaches the value you place on writing and thinking, penmanship and style. Because this endowment is seen as a traditional "rite of passage," the EverFlowing fountain pen becomes a child's daily touchstone, signifying that learning, knowledge, and creating are magnificent and special things. Keeping an EverFlowing pen at home for homework provides years of gratification, while making the statement your child is deserving of the best tools for her education.

In the Real World: Ads that missed their target:

Cleaning Lady - Tired of cleaning yourself? Let me do it.

Dog for sale: eats anything and is fond of children.

Now you try it

Try creating benefit statements for some of the other groups who are being ignored by the EverFlowing pen ad. Possibilities are listed at the end of this section, but give it a try before peeking.

1. Left-handed writers would wonder if all that nib bending worked for them.

_____

_____

_____

2. People with jewelry allergies, especially to silver, are out.

_____

_____

_____

_____

3. People who are frugal, "practical," or living on fixed incomes would see buying this pen as frivolous.

_____

_____

_____

_____

Sales Writing Tip:
Keeping the reader, or target market in mind is not enough in sales writing. You'll need to write the entire piece around the all-important issue of who your target market is.

Just remember: Benefits count only if the reader values those benefits from her own perspective.

4 It's never just about what *you* want!

I'll bet you've never seen an ad like this one:

Fly SuperGlobalWorld Airlines – We're desperately in need of cash, quickly.

Or a stock offering that said:

This investment involves risk. Read the entire prospectus before you invest. NEW-CORP needs capital instantly, as our officers have luxurious lifestyles that demand huge salaries.

The pros don't tell you what they want to take from you. They talk about something they have that you—their targeted audience—want or need.

Here are some samples where it's all about the "writer" instead of all about the "reader":

Our goal for this year's fundraiser is $100,000. If each employee contributed just $45, we'd meet our goal and purchase enough medicine to save over 2,200 needy children. Please be generous and think of those less fortunate than you during this year's drive.

Our budget for the year has been expended and no new replacements can be hired.

I'm writing to you because our department needs new computers.

All of the pieces above are essentially selling something, but each one was writer-focused. What's in it for the reader? Where is the benefit?

Here's a rewrite of the samples from above, switching from *writer-focused* to *reader-focused* copy. Notice that more words aren't needed to switch the **focus**, just a bit of thinking:

There's an opportunity for you to save a child's life during the next few minutes and feel the power of your personal generosity. If each employee contributed just $45, we'd meet our goal of $100,000, but regardless of how many employees contribute, each $45 gift will purchase enough medicine to save one child.

While our budget for the year has been expended, we believe hiring replacements will immediately generate profitability that will exceed their cost.

I'm writing to you because our department projects doubling productivity with new computers.

Now you try it

Pull up a recent short document you've written or received involving the sale of a concept, service, or item. We'll call this a "demo document."

Follow these steps;

- **Determine the focus.** Is it positioned from the reader's or writer's point of view? If it is from the writer's viewpoint, how would you shift the focus to the reader while better positioning the Power-selling points of costs, benefits, weight, and tracking?

- **Use an Idea Map.** Put the main idea in the middle, then add branches for costs, benefits, weight, and tracking. Place the phrases from your "demo document" onto your map.

- **Rewrite using your new sales writing skills!**

Good! You should be seeing clearer ways to sell already!

5 It's never about closing! It's always about the *reader* reaching her own conclusion.

Another common sales writing error is a shift from working with the reader to ordering the reader to buy or act. The whole goal of power-selling is to allow the reader to conclude that the benefits you're proposing outweigh the costs. If you cover the benefits, costs, and weight properly, but then shove a sales conclusion at your reader, the whole architectural integrity of the power-selling system becomes unstable. The reader feels duped and your carefully built argument comes tumbling down around you.

The elegance of this power-selling system lies in the fact that A (benefits), B (costs), and C (weight), lead to D (tracking). You need only to track or guide your reader to remember benefits, costs, and weight for your reader to come to the inevitable conclusion to act now.

Sales Writing Tip:
Avoid ordering your readers to act. Set the benefits stage, help them *weigh* those against the costs, and then *guide* them through the process of choosing your solution. When you're offering a win-win, it becomes natural and easy. If you're not offering a win-win, you're already in trouble.

The **old rules** of sales writing were:

*   *Tell 'em what you're gonna tell 'em*
*   *Tell 'em*
*   *Tell 'em what ya told 'em*
*   *Close 'em*

The **new rules** boil down to:

- Tell them quickly what's in it for them
- Help them understand why it's fair and mutually beneficial
- Guide them to come to their own conclusion

When you think in these terms and combine them with what you've learned so far, you give yourself a big advantage in your sales writing—right away.

Two more tools to superlative sales writing

Mastering two more tenets of sales-writing psychology (writing with directed goals and learning why people act on offers) will make your sales writing direct and effective. Lets look at both now.

Writing with Directed Goals

Writing your sales piece so readers come to their own conclusion to accept your offer makes sense. As you have seen, this is accomplished by successfully guiding your reader. To do that, you must create for yourself a very clear set of goals. Yet most people either ignore this important step or don't know how to go about it. Here are some examples of sales goals that *aren't* goals:

Close the deal.

I will sell more cars.

Have Jim in Finance approve our new corporate management bonus program.

Finish all my paperwork by Monday at noon.

What's wrong with these? None have the three essential components of a *directed* goal. And without those components, who knows if the goal will ever be reached?

Years ago I created this concept to help business owners and managers quickly create valid goals instead of wish lists.

1 **A directed goal incorporates all the elements for its attainment within a single statement that says:**

- What you want done
- When it will be done by
- What it will take to get it done

In a formula, a directed goal appears as:

2 *Some thing ("X") will happen by Some time ("Y") through* **the following** *actions ("Z")*.

Here are two examples of good directed goals made from the list above:

Close the deal might become:

I will close the Baker Mortgage deal by Wednesday through shopping their credit report to six more lenders, presenting the Bakers with the best rates, and locking in their choice of terms.

X is **close the Baker Mortgage**
Y is **Wednesday**
Z is **shopping their credit report to six more lenders, presenting the Bakers with the best rates, and locking in their choice of terms**

This directed goal now tells you what is happening, when, and by what means.

Let's try another example:

Have Jim in Finance approve our new corporate management bonus program.

might become:

*Jim in finance will approve our new corporate management bonus program , by October 1, — x
through my completion of the following tasks: — y
setting early meetings with Jim to get his input and parameters, gathering support from at least two other VP's in the form of letters from them — z
to Jim, creating the spreadsheet sample plans, writing up three examples of similar corporations with even more generous plans than my proposal and (prepared only as a last resort) getting my father, the president of the company, who has already guaranteed me his support, to insist on approval.*

This directed goal states everything the writer will need to do to effect the desired outcome.

Just looking at the last directed goal, can you imagine what the branches of an Idea Map might look like? You can use Idea Maps to give structure to your directed goals and help you with your sales writing.

Sales Writing Tip:
By adding a directed goal to your sales writing, you dramatically increase the probability of your reader accepting your offer.

✒ Practice: Sales writing practice #5

Turn the following into directed goals:

1. Finish all my paperwork by Monday at noon.

I will finish all my paperwork by Monday at noon,
by doing

_____

_____

_____

2. Close the deal. (Use a real one if you have one
    brewing.)

_____

_____

_____

_____

_____

Effective sales writing always begins with a writer's intention or goal. Now you have the formula and skills for writing goals that state what you want, when you want it, and how you will achieve it—Directed Goals!

Now let's move to the final concept of this section, and my personal favorite: why people actually choose to act on offers and how to use this sales knowledge in your writing.

Sales Writing Psychology:
Why People Act on Offers

People will act on an offer for reasons too numerous to count. Just look at the hundreds of books on the subject covering everything from reptilian impulses to the influence of color on store purchases. But some irrefutable concepts lie at the base of all good selling, and I want to arm you with some of these so you can apply them to your sales writing every day.

First, though, I'd like to take you on a little illustrative journey. Included with this book is a pair of Prismatic Novalogic® glasses. You'll need these for this exercise.

CAUTION: Removal and Care of the Included Prismatic Novalogic® Glasses, attached to the back cover of this book:

Turn to the inside back cover and carefully remove the glasses from their bound, cardboard case. Don't scratch them or place your fingers on the lenses. Put on the glasses and allow a couple of seconds for your eyes to adjust before focusing on the image in the center of the box below.

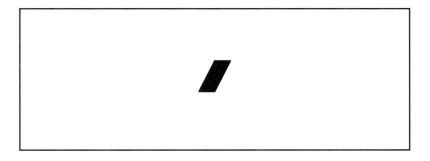

If you've flipped to the back of the book looking for the glasses, or are curious if glasses are included with this book, that's good. It means you have imagination and have been persuaded to take the course of action the writer intended. Even though you've been holding this book for a while and you consciously know no "real" glasses are included, you are following (or considering following) active directions.

Why would we look for glasses we know aren't there? Because most of us will follow or accept—to some level—authoritarian statements, especially if they appeal to our sense of imagination or fun. But more deeply rooted is the desire to believe in the positive on a guttural level.

Sales Writing Tip:
Increase positive response to your sales writing by adding appropriate excitement, differences, or benefits.

By using the glasses example here, I'm not demonstrating good selling technique. I'm making the point that most of us want to believe in something fun, beneficial, or exciting.

How can you use this in your everyday sales writing? Color your writing, where it works, with imagery. Take a look:

Guided imagery

Which statement makes you more likely to consider purchasing insurance if you have a family?

Picture This:

"I am a passenger on spaceship earth."

-R. Buckminster Fuller

a. *Risk is an inherent part of liv-ing. You have a wife and chil-dren. You have a responsibility to provide for them both now and throughout the future of their lives. But the reality is that at any moment something unforeseen can happen to you which could disable you or even take your life. Rare diseases, cancer, heart attack, and accidents all happen to real people every day. We're all mortal. So do you ignore the risk or do you do something about it? You can mitigate risk by properly insuring your life, which provides assistance to your loved ones in times of loss.*

For just about $200 a month, a nonsmoking male, age 35, can purchase a million-dollar life policy. Shouldn't you consider the peace of mind that kind of insurance would bring to your family?

b. *Sally jumped down from her pony, her face all lit up with a smile, as she tossed off one of those babbling-brook, infectious giggles her father had loved so much. Mark would have been at his little girl's 7th birthday party, had he not been stricken with a rare, terminal blood disease just four months ago.*

When Mark turned 35 years old, he discussed the future with his wife Ellie. Together, they decided to trim their family entertainment and clothing budgets by just about $7 a day to invest in a comprehensive insurance program with a million dollars in benefits to cover catastrophic loss. While nothing can replace the loss of her daddy, Sally and her mom will be financially secure for the rest of their lives, thanks to Mark's insurance program.

Most people are motivated by "b" to consider buying insurance for the simple reason the story uses imagery to help them visualize their own potential loss. They *become* part of the story. They

Picture This:

Life is like a 10 speed bike. Most of us have gears we never use.

-Charles M. Schultz, creator of "Peanuts"

can feel the pain they'll suffer if they don't buy insurance and the relief and security they'll enjoy if they do. The "a" example evokes almost no imagery, instead using dry concepts and complex words that require the reader to work to create a story through word interpretation.

Using words to illustrate tangible concepts to invoke the five senses—making "movies in the mind"—represents a form of sales and marketing psychology based on **guided imagery**.

Let's look at some less dramatic examples. The first in each set avoids any imagery or expectation of benefit or fun. The second uses tangible concepts (invoking the movies in the reader's mind) to help sell the statement. The second statement is the better choice in each case:

"Written words are far more powerful than implements of conflict."

or

"The pen is mightier than the sword."

And another:

"Thanks for your order. You qualify for a 10% discount on future orders placed through our Internet site within 10 days. Check out our new assortment of clove honey, classic gift bags, and wine."

or

"Thanks for your order. CLICK HERE for your 10% discount on new orders placed through our Cinematic Web site within 10 days. See 10-second movies of our gift-wrapped "sticky" clove honey, classic "picnic" gift bags, and assortment of sparkling and red wines."

And this one:

The Korean division meeting is confirmed. The meeting is scheduled for Wednesday at noon. Please bring technical items that assist you in the workplace to share with the group. A 15-minute period for unstructured meeting time where team members can interact and share their technology has been set aside.

or

Our division will meet our Korean counterparts Wednesday at noon. Please bring handheld computers, minirecorders, or anything super-tech that assists you in the workplace to share with the group. We'll enjoy a 15-minute open-group session where both groups will pair off, demo their gear, and make new friends.

Sales Writing Tip:
You gain an incremental benefit by creating movies in the reader's mind whenever circumstances permit.

Pushing buttons

In Chapter Two, Dr. Miller tells you to use words to paint pictures in your writing. For sales writing, I'll go further and tell you to use those word-pictures to *evoke emotions* wherever possible. In sales psychology, I call this kind of guided imagery **pushing buttons**.

The human brain has trouble differentiating between emotions we feel as a result of real events in our lives and emotions evoked through art. That's why we cry when we read a heart-wrenching novel, feel a rush of adrenaline while watching a suspense film, fall in love with the sweet ingénue in a play, get mad as hell when the hero of the TV show suffers injustice. The intensity of these emotions is just as strong as those we feel in real life.

You can't use this tool to fool your reader, but you can use it to help her understand your point better, to connect with you, and to heighten the desire for your offering.

Here is a list of questions to ask yourself about *button pushing*. In the follow questions, "it" will refer to your offering, product, or concept.

- How does it feel?
- What would you feel if you touched it?
- How does it look that relates to something emotional?
- Does it have a scent reminiscent of something?
- Is a sound associated with it that reminds you of something else?
- Does it have any taste or flavor that you could describe to whet the appetite of your reader?
- How could you animate the objects you're discussing to allow for a sound, smell, taste, feeling?

The difficulty lies, not in the new ideas, but in escaping the old ones, which ramify, for those brought up as most of us have been, into every corner of our minds.

–John Maynard Keynes

Keeping this list in mind, let's take a look at some copy from *Travel & Leisure Magazine* describing Hungarian castles:

Mention staying the night in a European castle and travelers are sure to have visions of the mansions of French kings and Spanish moors: canopied beds, well-trained valets, Aubusson tapestries. The castle hotels of Hungary are a species apart. Though slightly less luxurious than their western European counterparts, they nonetheless provide a rare opportunity to indulge in a rich man's vacation at a poor man's price.

Now I'll rewrite this with the goal of emotional button pushing. When you write to push the reader's buttons, your copy will necessarily be longer than if you're giving them "just the facts." Not only must you provide the essential information, but you need to create the imagery that stirs emotions:

The candlelight chandeliers flicker and shadows take on life-like forms on the ceilings, the walls and the floors. Somewhere a creaking door echoes through the hallways. European castle hotels, with their stately demeanor and luxurious appointments, never fail to stir the imagination and bring out the royalty in all of us. The castle hotels of Hungary are a species apart. Nearly as luxurious as their European counterparts, they provide the thrill of castle living for a fraction of the European cost. Place your hand on a rough stone wall or a fine thousand-year-old tapestry and you're instantly transformed into a king or queen. There's a fragrant yet musty scent, different in every Hungarian castle, but clearly a mark of the passage of time. Best of all, the Hungarian castle provides a more romantic experience as the rooms and staff depart from the traditional European rigidity in favor of local custom and color. Sink into a hot bath once used by a noble knight and let the waters of centuries gone by ease the tensions of the modern day. Celebrate your Hungarian castle vacation in royal style while saving a king's ransom.

You may find it easier to push buttons with tangible objects (like pens and castles) than with pure concepts. However, if you review the example on insurance provided earlier, paying attention to the emotions evoked with Sally and her pony, you'll see the same concepts at work.

Practice: Sales writing practice #6

Take out a recent letter, memo, or proposal and see if you can find one place where you could add a statement that reinforces your proposition while pushing a button. Can you find a second place that makes sense? How about a third reinforcement with button pushing? Push as many buttons as you feel necessary to help the reader emotionally experience your benefits and you'll enjoy a better response. Just be careful not to go overboard!

Here's an idea to help get you started. Circle the adjectives and adverbs in your writing sample, then go to the thesaurus and look them up. You will find similar words you can use that might push the reader's buttons more effectively.

Another helpful hint: Try reading a movie or TV script once a month. (You can find these by searching the Internet.) By definition, these scripts are written to push the buttons of their audience. Regularly reviewing samples like these genres will help you not only see what kind of words and phrasing the pros use to push buttons, but get you into the habit of writing that way yourself.

Play it again, Sam!

If you really want to see an immediate improvement in your sales writing, I urge you to reread this entire section, even skim it, before actually applying the concepts to your documents. Here's why: To help you hone in on your own potential sales writing errors, I wrote this section in an "inverse" manner. Concepts are given, errors uncovered, and then deeper understanding discussed. Now that you've been through the "ah-ha" process, you'll become a much better sales writer if you start at the top and read this section again, armed with your new knowledge. You'll find it refreshing, stimulating, and very reinforcing. I hope you take the short time to do this!

In Summary

We've covered a lot of ground in this section which collectively will make your sales writing stronger.

- You clearly understand the difference between writing for **communication** and writing for **selling**.

- Sales writing can be broken down into two categories: the selling of a **product or service** or the selling of an **idea** or the **writer's position**.

- In my **power-selling**, communication leads to a desired action within your timeframe.

- The new sales theory is based on **guided teamwork leading to mutually beneficial results,** with the salesperson functioning as the conductor of the team.

- Your sales writing should always have a **win-win intention and outcome**.

- **Using the power-selling concept,** you guide your reader to conclude what you're offering is worth more than the cost you're asking, so that the reader makes his own decision to take (or move closer to) your recommended action.

- You know how to incorporate the **power-selling concepts** of **benefits, costs, weight, and tracking into your sales writing.**

- Five dangers of visiting "Neverland" are:
  1. It's **never** *just* about the *price*!
  2. It's **never** about *features.* It's **always** about *benefits*!
  3. It's **never** about the *benefits themselves.* It's **always** about *how* the *reader perceives* the *benefits*!
  4. It's **never** just about what *you* want!
  5. It's **never** about *closing*! It's **always** about the *reader reaching her own conclusion.*

- For any sales writing, you learned **you must have a specific directed goal,** stated as: *Some thing* ("X") will happen by *some time* ("Y") *through* the following *actions* ("Z").

- We explored the importance of using **sales psychology,** which involves **the suggestion of something exciting, different, or novel.**

- **We discussed the value of adding guided imagery, movies of the mind, and pushing buttons to enhance your sales writing.**

Answers to Practice Questions

✎ Practice: Sales writing practice #3

The EverFlowing line of fountain pens offer pure silver barrels, with 24K gold nibs and broad points. Unlike today's trend towards disposable, inexpensive, plastic writing tools the EverFlowing line offers a <u>serious, heavier, satisfying feeling</u>. European hand-craftsmanship renders each pen <u>a unique masterpiece</u>. Only 24K gold is used for our nibs as <u>the gold's softness allows the nib to bend and conform to each user's writing style—and soon become an "old friend."</u> Our broad points are the hallmark of an EverFlowing pen, <u>providing commanding boldness</u> and <u>satisfying flow</u> to <u>every stroke, every word, every thought</u>. The simple act of removing the cap and exposing the glistening point, or of seating the cap on the barrel end with a distinctive snap, <u>reminds the owner he or she is important, privileged,</u> and certainly <u>worthy of the finer things in life.</u> To hold an EverFlowing pen <u>is to instantly experience the anticipation of the great writing which simply must issue forth from a writing instrument of this caliber.</u>

✎ Practice: Sales writing practice #4

1. Left-handed writers would wonder if all that nib bending worked for them. Possible benefit statement: *Our gold nibs are equally well suited for shaping to the style of both left- and right-handed writers.*

2. People with jewelry allergies, especially to silver, are out. Possible benefit statement: *The pure silver barrels, layered with a coat of your favorite clear, acrylic nail polish, become instantly hypo-allergenic for those sensitive to direct contact with silver.*

3. People who are frugal, "practical," or living on fixed incomes would see buying this pen as frivolous. Possible benefit statement: *EverFlowing pens enjoy an average life of 50 years. Census results indicate consumers purchase 5 disposable pens annually, the purchase of an EverFlowing pen saves money over time while offering exceptionally reliable service.*

APPENDIX

A Handy Reader Meter
242

Transitions
243

The Steps: From Idea to Article
245

You Want Answers?
249

References by Chapter
251

Additional Source Books
255

Index
257

About the Authors & Special Resources
271

A Handy Reader Meter

This *Reader Meter* can help you understand your reader. Where does yours fit on this meter? Is your message focused on your reader or yourself? Think about what classification *he/she* may fall into. Depending on the purpose of the document, your approach may change.

Reader	Purpose of Message	Best Approach
Someone outside the field: w/no or limited knowledge	• General interest/ understanding of information	• Simple, short explanations and concrete examples, stories/anecdotes • Limited or no tech. lang. • Limited theory
Executive: Makes decisions & solves probs.	• Makes decisions about resources, products, services, & personnel	• Use little/no technical lang. advantages • Emphasize: Market potential of prod. alternative approaches, costs, & results
Specialist: Expert in field	• Wants/needs new information, opinions, data, techniques, theories • Analytical conclusions, results • Write in specialist lang.	• Little background • Factual information w/o judgment/opinions • Thorough methodology • Well-defined bibliography
Technician: Person who builds, maintains, services equipment/ programs	• Needs information to maintain or troubleshoot, operate, understand equipment, programs, service	• Little theory • Info. that is practical, useful in simple format • Use a "how to" approach • Picture, graphs, charts
Operator: Carries out instructions	• Needs information to operate equipment, programs, or services	• Simple, sequential, & detailed steps • Visuals, pictures

Transitions

Reference from Chapter Three.

- **To guide the reader:** First, second, third, next, one, besides, then, before, after, finally, meanwhile, later, soon, formerly, afterward, until now, since, again, immediately, today, in the past, recently, earlier, moreover, furthermore, to begin with, above all, also, best of all, more important

- **To introduce an example:** For example, for instance, to explain, specifically, to contrast, to describe, to compare, to refute, in other words, to support, to illustrate, to define, for instance, consequently, as an illustration

- **To add a fact, a thought, an idea:** Also, and, besides, finally, furthermore, again, moreover, next, too, as well as, in addition to, since, that is, in fact, then, similarly, additionally, another, it's true that

- **To alert reader to change in thought:** Moreover, on the contrary, however, but, nevertheless, on the other hand, the fact remains that, equally important, unfortunately

- **To conclude:** All in all, to conclude, in conclusion, to summarize, finally, last of all, therefore, in summary, the point is, as one can see, in short, for these reasons, to sum up, as a result, in other words, to review, I conclude that, in closing, to close, briefly

- **To compare, contrast, show cause and effect:** But, however, on the other hand, on the contrary, although, nevertheless, instead, as a result, therefore, because, consequently, yet, still, or, even so, similarly, likewise, still, actually, conversely, in contrast, rather

- **To show purpose:** To this end, for this purpose, for this reason, with this objective in mind, because of

- **To show condition or consequence:** Provided, providing, on condition, in any case, subject to, whether, if, with the stipulation, with the understanding, in either case, accordingly, subsequently

- **To show spatial order or direction:** Above, below, here, there, outside, inside, nearby, beyond, over, under, across, on the left, right, close, then, next

The Steps: From Idea to Article

1 *Time Management Habits* Idea Map

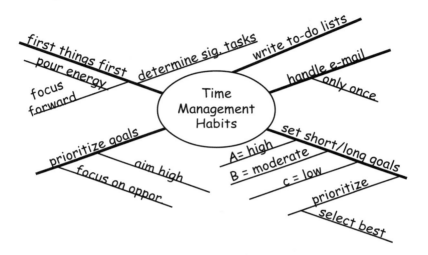

2 *Time Management Habits* Power Structure
Power 1=time management habits
    Power 2= do first things first
        Power 3=determine significant tasks
            Power 4=pour your energy
        Power 3=focus on forward movement
    Power 2=prioritize goals
        Power 3=focus on opportunity
        Power 3=aim high
    Power 2=write to-do lists
    Power 2=set short/long goals
        Power 3=prioritize by level of importance
            Power 4=select for best results
    Power 2=handle e-mails
        Power 3=only once!
Power 1=make time work

3 Time Management Habits Power 1 and 2 sentences

Power 1=Practicing five indispensable habits is your passbook to a full and rich life.
Power 2=Do first things first.
Power 2=Prioritizing your goals is the second habit.
Power 2=A third habit consists of writing to-do lists.
Power 2=Set short- and long-range goals.
Power 2=Learn how to handle the slew of e-mails that arrive each day.
Power 1=Make time work.

4 Time Management Habits converted into Power 1 and Power 2 paragraphs

Practicing five indispensable time management habits can be your passbook to a full and rich life.

Start by focusing on first things first. By determining the most significant work for you to accomplish, you narrow your concentration to a few activities that get results. Since not enough time is available to do everything, choose the most important tasks and pour your energy into those.

Second, prioritize your goals. Your goals must be centered on opportunities rather than past failures. Only through ranking your objectives will you achieve focus.

A third habit consists of writing to-do lists. Goal-oriented people always write things down. By doing so, goals become more than just ideas. Writing makes them real.

Fourth, setting short- and long-range goals should become an ingrained habit. This process consists of deciding what level of importance each of them has. Then organize the tasks around completing your goals.

Last, learning how to handle the slew of e-mails that arrive each day is imperative. Touching the same message more than once wastes an inordinate amount of time.

Making time work for you remains the most important habit you can acquire in today's extraordinarily busy world.

5 *Time Managment Habits* converted into news-letter article with Power 1, 2, and 3 paragraphs

Imagine a bank that makes an $86,400 deposit daily into your account, but with a slight hitch—the balance does not carry over and the account returns to zero every night. Time is the same way: You have 86,400 seconds daily to spend any way you wish. They, too, do not carry over to the next day. How you manage those all-too-precious seconds and minutes will determine the quality of your life. Practicing five indispensable time management habits can be your passbook to a full and rich life.

Start by focusing on first things first. By determining the most significant work for you to accomplish, you narrow your concentration to a few activities that get results. Since not enough time is available to do everything, choose the most significant tasks and pour your energy into those.

Repeating this daily mantra—I must do *first things first*—forces you to home in on important work and eliminate those tasks that don't move you forward.

Second, prioritize your goals. They must be centered on opportunities rather than past failures. Only through ranking your objectives will you achieve focus.

Focusing on future opportunities should drive the organization. You can't change what's happened; you can only prepare for what will happen. That's where your energy and attention must be   directed—outward towards success. Remember to always aim high!

A third habit consists of writing to-do lists. Goal-oriented people always write things down. By doing so, goals become more than just ideas. Writing goals down makes them real, concrete, and attainable.

Fourth, setting short- and long-range goals should become an ingrained habit. This process consists of deciding what level of importance each goal has. Then organize your tasks around completing the goals.

Label these tasks A, B, and C. *A* tasks always get picked, as they will create results. Those tasks labeled **B** are placed in a file that says "pending," while the **C** tasks are put in a drawer that may read "when hell freezes over." Translation: No time or energy should be spent on **C** tasks.

Last, learning how to handle the slew of e-mails that arrives each day is imperative. Touching the same message more than once wastes an inordinate amount of time.

It would stagger the imagination to consider how many times you review the same e-mail before you act on it. Force yourself to make a decision about each piece of correspondence *the first time*. Will you file it, delete it, or respond to it? Choose.

Anyone can acquire these five habits. Simple, tested, and proven in the real world of work, they help you accomplish more—in less time, thus freeing you for enjoyable pursuits. Making time work for you remains the most important habit you can acquire in today's extraordinarily busy world.

You Want Answers?

Chapter Two:

Power Quizzes - pages 50-52
#1Power Sentences 1 2 3 2 3
#2Power Sentences 1 2 2 2 2 2 2
#3Power Sentences 1 2 3 4 2 3
#4Power Paragraphs 1 2 3 4 2 3 3

Chapter Three:

Power Quizzes - page 65
0 0 1 2 2 3 2 3

Pedantic Phrases - page 81
2. Your letter stated
3. Your instructions state
4. Whether
5. Say yes
6. Because
7. Soon

Power Quizzes - pages 84-85
#2 Power Sentences 1 2 3 3 4
#4 Power Sentences 1 2 3 2 3 4 2 3 1

Chapter Four:

Page 91
2. Thank you for the opportunity to assist you. We believe we can help you show a profit by changing your marketing approach.
3. To make changes, please first apply to the appropriate department. Also, I've attached the manual regarding deregulations. Please sign, date and return it to this office by May XXXX.

4. Due to high demand for our Platinum Plan, we need to adjust rates effective July XXXX.

Page 93
1. You'll find scads of scanners on the market, and some are really inexpensive.
2. Each 911 call has legal ramifications.
3. The technology sector has three good stock buys.
4. Our department wrote a lot of grants.
5. "Medical eligibility" has a clear definition.
6. Much about digital photography is cool.
7. Expect lots more before the dust settles.

Page 96
1. The committee studied the situation.
2. This company sells insurance.
3. To keep our program running, our managers use evaluation tools.
4. Good writing involves hard work.
5. Proposal "C" costs less.

Redundant Phrases - page 109
1. final
2. 4:00 p.m
3. problems
4. cooperate
5. immediately
6. strategy
7. commute

References By Chapter

Chapter One

Buzan, Tony. *Use Both Sides of Your Brain*. New York: Dutton, 1976.
Drucker, Peter F. *The Effective Executive*. New York: Harper Row, 1966.
Hyerle, David. *Visual Tools for Constructing Knowledge*. Alexandria: ASCD, 1996.
Lakekin, Alan. *How to Get Control of Your Life and Your Time*. New York: P. H. Wyden, 1973.
O'Conner, Patricia. *Words Fail Me*. New York: Harcourt Brace and Company, 1999.
Rico, Gabriele. *Writing the Natural Way*. Los Angeles: Tarcher, 1983.
Wheatley, Margaret J. *Leadership and the New Science: Learning about Organization from an Orderly Universe*. San Franciso: Berrett-Koehler Publishers, Inc, 1992.

Chapter Two

Adaptation of Power Numbers system from earlier works of Socrates (469-399 BC); Hayakawa (1947) Sparks (1982); Christiansen (1979).
Lederer, Richard. *Get Thee to a Punnery*. Charleston: Wyrick and Company, 1988.

Chapter Three

Feedback questions adapted from "Writing YOUR Natural Way," Fairfax Station, Virginia: *The Type Reporter*, 1990.
Barzun, Jacques. *Simple and Direct: Rhetoric for Writers*. New York: Harper & Row, 1975.
Brusaw, Charles T., Alred, Gerald J., Oliu, Walter E. *Handbook of Technical Writing*. New York: St. Martin's Press, 1993.
Cheney, Theodore A. Rees. *Getting the Words Right: How to Revise, Edit and Rewrite*. Cincinnati: Writer's Digest Books, 1983.
Elbow, Peter. *Writing with Power: Techniques for Mastering the Writing Process*. Cincinnati: Oxford University Press, 1981.
Lutz, William. *The New Doublespeak*. New York: Harper Collins, 1996.
O'Conner, Patricia. *Words Fail Me*. New York: Harcourt Brace and Company, 1999.
Saltzman, Joel. *If You Can Talk, You Can Write*. New York: Warner Books, 1993.
Zinsser, Willliam. *On Writing Well*. New York: Harper-Perennial, 1990.

Chapter Four

Andersen, Richard. *Writing That Works*. New York: McGraw-Hill, 1989.

Brohaugh, William. *Write Tight: How to Keep Your Prose Sharp, Focused and Concise*. Cincinnati: Writer's Digest Books, 1993.

Brusaw, Charles T., Alred, Gerald J., Oliu, Walter E. *Handbook of Technical Writing*. New York: St. Martin's Press, 1993.

Hamilton, Betty. *The 3 Steps to Powerful Writing*. Adrian, Michigan: C & C Graphics, 1997.

Lederer, Richard. *Anguished English*. Charleston: Wyrick and Company, 1987.

Lederer, Richard. *Get Thee to a Punnery*. Charleston: Wyrick and Company, 1988.

Chapter Five

Emarketer, 2003. http://www.emarketer.com

Fogiel, M. *Research and Education Association's Handbook of English Grammer, Style, and Writing*. Piscataway: REA, 1994.

MSNBC, February 2003.

McKinnon, Wayne. *Wayne McKinnon's Complete Guide to E-mail*. Ontario: Ryshell Books, 1999.

Neilsen's NetRatings, February 2003.

O'Conner, Patricia. *Woe Is I*. New York: Riverhead Books, 2002.

O'Conner, Patricia. *Words Fail Me*. New York: Harcourt Brace and Company, 1999.

Pew Internet and American Life Project, 2002. http://www.pewinternet.org

Venolia, Jan. *Write Right! A Desktop Digest of Punctuation, Grammar, and Style*. Berkeley: Ten Speed Press, 1979.

Chapter Six

Goodwin, Kathleen, *B-Blogs Cause a Stir*, February 3, 2003, ClickzExperts, http://www.clickz.com/experts/em_mkt/enl_strat/article.php/1579091.

Lederer, Richard. *Anguished English*. Charleston: Wyrick and Company, 1987.

McKinnon, Wayne. *Wayne McKinnon's Complete Guide to E-mail*. Ontario: Ryshell Books, 1999.

Weil, Debbie, *Top 20 Definitions of Blogging*, December 9, 2003, MarketingProfs.com, http://www.marketingprofs.com/login/signup.asp?source=/3/weil9.asp.

Weil, Debbie, *To Blog or Not to Blog. . .That's a Good Question*, August 22, 2001, ClickzExperts, http://www.clickz.com/experts/em_mkt/b2b_em_mkt/print.php/870481.

Appendix

Reader Meter adapted from Thomas Pearsall, *Audience Analysis for Technical Writing*. Beverly Hills: Glencoe Press, 1969.

Source Books Suggested by the Authors

Dr. Julie Miller

I find having the following books in my library to be of tremendous help. James J. Kilpatrick's *The Art of Writing* (Andrews and Mcmeel) is useful with his examples taken from current print. Brusaw, Alred, and Oliu's *Handbook of Technical Writing* (St. *Martin's Press)* is an extensive text and well worth having. If you enjoy Richard Lederer's humor (*Anguished English; Get Thee to a Punnery*), you may also want to take a peek at William Safire's numerous titles on our mother tongue. Author Patricia T. O'Conner's books are a primer on how to write with humor. Here are other books you may find useful.

Gordon, Karen Elizabeth, *The Deluxe Transitive Vampire*, Pantheon Books, New York, 1993.

Judd, Karen, *Copyediting*, Crisp Publications, Inc., Los Altos, CA, 1990.

A Manual of Style, 15th Edition Revision, The University of Chicago Press, Chicago, 2004.

Nurnberg, Maxwell, *Questions You Always Wanted to Ask About English*, Washington Square Press, Pocket Books, New York, 1972.

Sabin, William A., *The Gregg Reference Manual*, Tenth Edition, Glencoe/McGraw-Hill Book Company, New York, 2004.

Shertzer Margaret, *The Elements of Grammar*, Macmillian Publishing Company, New York, 1986.

Strunk, William, Jr., and E.B. White, *The Elements of Style*, 4th Edition, Macmillan Publishing Co, Inc, New York, 1999.

Sullivan, K.D., *Go Ahead…Proof It!*, Barron's, Hauppage, New York, 1996.

The American Heritage Dictionary, Third Edition, Houghton Mifflin Company, Boston, 2000.

Truss, Lynne, *Eats. Shoots & Leaves*, Gotham Books, New York, 2004.

Walsh, Bill, *Lapsing into a Comma*, McGraw-Hill/Contemporary Books, New York, 2000.

Jonathan Todd

The following is an eclectic but well rounded library of books to assist the writer looking for a sales and marketing edge. First is *Business Writing That Counts!* by Dr. Julie Miller (Hara Publishing). You already have this book but I'll encourage you to reread it annually. Julie's form leads to clear, clean writing which always produces greater selling potential. While the rest of my selections for you are not about "writing" they will each spur you on to write better sales material in a particular way. The first (and oldest) is a gem published in 1958 by Richard Irwin, Inc., called *Cases In Marketing Strategy* written by Richard M. Clewett, Ralph Westfall and Harper W. Boyd, Jr. The section on "Selling and Advertising" allows current day sellers to see what is and isn't working after nearly half a century. Model the stuff that still works! Possibly my favorite book to spur great sales writing is *The 48 Laws of Power* by Robert Greene and Joost Elffers (Viking). While the authors didn't intend this to be a sales writing text, the brilliant psychology they share is instantly applicable to honing your sales writing. Another great writing companion is *The Portable MBA* by Eliza G. C. Collins and Mary Anne Devanna (Wiley). Reviewing the section "Becoming a Marketing Driven Company" is especially helpful for writing good sales material because of the authors' clear explanation of how consumers react to marketing and sales. *Hardball* by Robert L. Shook (Morrow) is a great read for those of you who sell for a living. For those of you embarking on a sales writing journey via the Internet, the *E-Business Legal Handbook* by Michael Rustad and Cyrus Daftary has the legal nuts and bolts for writers in this relatively new field.

INDEX

A

accuracy, 187
acronyms, avoiding, 100–101, 170, 183
action words, 69
active voice, 94–95, 97, 98, 183
adjectives and adverbs, use of, 108
analogies, 103, 105
Andrews, Paul, 100
Anguished English (Lederer), 104–105
apostrophe, 137, 138
application letters, 69
appositives, 131
audience, target, 57, 58, 189, 217–218, 219. *See also* reader

B

Bankhead, Tallulah (quote), 138
Barzun, Jacques (quote), 75
B-Blogs, 188
Beckett, Samuel (quote), 115
beginnings, document, 56–58
    suggestions for, 62–64
Bel Air, Candace Kovner, 164
benefits and benefit statements, 200–221, 240
    reader-focused, 64, 206, 207–208, 221, 222, 224
    in sales, 215, 216, 217, 218–219. *See also* cost-benefit
Bennett, Arnold (quote), 131
Bernanke, Dr. Ben, 48
Bernstein, Theodore (quote), 95
Bird by Bird (Lamott), 39
bird walk(s), 22, 33, 41, 96
blogs, 188–189
body of document, 66
brainstorming, 8, 9–10
Brautigan, Richard (quote), 67
brevity, 124, 186
Britt, S. (quote), 158
Brock, Lou (quote), 105

Brown, Mike, e-mails, 177
Buchanan, Pat, 103
Buchwald, Art, 131
business. *See also* Sales writing
    letters, 150–151. *See also* letters
    writing, 199

C

Cabell, James Branch (quote), 131
capitalization, 139–140
Cervantes, Miguel de (quote), 135
Cheever, John (quote), 9
Chicago Manual of Style, 74
chunking information, 144
Churchill, Winston (quote), 120
Cicero (quote), 154
clarity, 90
        in blogs, 189
        rewriting for, 90-91, 98
        simplifying for, 90
        tip, 124
C.L.E.V.R. solutions, 89, 128, 183
clichés, 99–100
closing, document, 55
colon, 132–133
color, use of, 149
commas, 129–132, 134
communication
    blogs as means of, 188
    clarity in, 91
    common vocabulary for, 22–23
    by Internet / e-mail, 1, 175–176, 179
    letters as, 149
    memos as, 148–149
    online sales, 161
    writing for, 237
Complete Guide to E-Mail, 186
Complete Idiot's Guide to Office Politics, 186
Concluding Power 1, 23
conclusions, document, 86. *See also* endings
    in professional reports, 167
    tips for, 70

contractions, in writing, 120, 137–138
Cook, Marshall (quote), 55
cost-benefit analysis in sales, 206, 207–208, 209, 212, 224, 237
cover letters, 106
cover sheets for faxes, 189, 190
Coward, Noel (quote), 147
creativity, in Idea Mapping, 5–6, 11, 25
customer service, 162
Cut to the Chase Marketing Web site (Wagner), 161–162

D

dash, 134–135
DeVries, Peter, 39
directed goals (in sales writing), 225–228, 238
document. *See also* letters
    body of, 66
    closing/ending, 55, 66
    design guidelines, 143–145
    formatting, 142
    opening/beginning, 55–56
    purpose of, 9, 58, 66, 71
    tone of, 57
    types of, 56–57
Doublespeak (Lutz), 81
drafts
    checking, 66
    combining sentences, 115
    expanding, 47
    reworking/refining, 71, 73–75
    tip, 110
    transitions in, 83, 86
    writing, 38–39
    Zero Power sentences in, 62

E

E-biz writing, 175
e-blasts, 178
editing, 122
    marks, 123
    tip, 124
Elbow, Peter (quote), 87

Elements of Style, 73
e-mail, 175
    checklist, 187
    concluding sentence or paragraph in, 69
    dos and don'ts, 184–185
    example, 180
    handling (example), 47
    managing, 185
    protocol, 176–179
    signatures, 84, 177–178
    tips, 162
    writing, 148
emoticons, 178
endings, document, 66–68
    practice writing, 70
executive summary, 169–170, 173
    example, 171–172

F

A Farewell to Arms, 71
faxing, 189–190
feedback, 121–122, 182
five W's, 163–164
Flaubert, Gustave (quote), 106
font size and style, 144
format(ting), 142
    of proposal, 173
Fowler, Gene (quote), 1
France, Anatole (quote), 82
free-writing, 23, 37
Fuller, R. Buckminster (quote), 230

G

Gabor, Zsa Zsa (quote), 135
Galbraith, John Kenneth, 132
Gates, Bill (quote), 131
Get Thee to a Punnery (quotes), 133, 137
getting started, 3–4, 25
Gingold, Hermione (quote), 129
goals
    in sales and sales writing, 203, 225–228, 238

writing (example), 44, 46
Goldwyn, Samuel (quote), 135
Goodman, Walter (quote), 103
grant writers and writing, 75, 76
    tip, 175
Greenspan, Alan (quote), 80
Gregg Reference Manual, example, 74, 95, 138
group writing, 74
guided imagery, 230–233, 238

H

Hamlet quote, 98
Handbook of Technical Writing, 105, 169
Hawking, Professor Stephen, 103
Hemingway, Ernest (quote), 71
Holmes, Oliver Wendell (quote), 98
Hubbard, Kim (quote), 138
hyphens, 138–139

I

I / me, downplaying, 158
Idea Map, 23, 25. *See also* power numbering
    charting your own, 7, 21
    example of, 7
    in group, 74
    mapping questions, 9, 10, 12, 16, 17 (example), 23
    for organization of ideas, 4, 25
    performance review example, 14
    practice, 15
    in professional reports, 166
    for proposals, 173
    reasons for/ purposes of, 22
    for sales writing, 159, 216, 217, 223, 227
    steps in, 8–12, 245–248 (Appendix)
    time management habits, 8, 10, 11, 12 (Figures 1–4)
    tips for, 7, 8, 15
imagery, guided, 230–233, 238
immediacy, demand for, 2
infinitives, split, 120
informational writing, 52
Internet. *See also* e-mail

communication, 1, 161, 175, 179
    immediacy of, 2
introductions, 55, 56, 86. *See also* beginnings
italics, 136

J

Jacobson, Peggy, 142, 169
jargon, 100, 170, 183
Johnson, Samuel (quote), 113

K

Keynes, John Maynard, 234
Kidder, Tracy, 52
Kilpatrick, James (quotes), 79, 103, 105
King, Martin Luther, Jr. (quote), 134

L

Lamb, Charles (quote), 155
Lamott, Anne (quote), 39
Landrum, Rita, 105
language
    biased, 101, 183
    guide to plain, 78
    sexist, 101
    user-friendly, 76
Lederer, Richard, 104
letters, 149–155. *See also* sales letters
    "bad news," 154–155
    business, 150–151
    complaint / claims, 155–158, 198
    conclusions in, 69
    cover, 106
    do's and don'ts, 152–153
    "good news," 153–154
    handwritten, 163
    thank-you, 162–163
Lieberman, Wendy (quote), 129
Lutz, William, 81

M

mapping question, 9, 10, 12, 16, 17 (example), 23
market, target, 218, 219–220, 221. *See also* sales writing
Marx, Chico (quote), 135
Marx, Groucho (quote), 150
McKinnon, Wayne, 186, 189
memos, 69, 148–149
Merriam-Webster Dictionary (quote), 197
metaphors, 103, 104
Michalko, Michael (quote), 15
Michener, James, 39
misspellings, 141–142
MLA Style Manual and Guide to Scholarly Publishing, 74
mnemonic, 23, 89
Molière (quote), 62

N

Nash, Ogden (quote), 130
neologisms, 119
newsletters, writing conclusions to, 70
news/press releases, 69
niche markets, 219
note-taking, 22
nouns, use of, 102–103, 108

O

O'Conner, Patricia T. (quotes), 48, 176, 177
O'Neill, Eugene, 138
one-legged interview, 169
online messages, 161. *See also* e-mail; Internet
opening, document, 55. *See also* beginnings
opinion, molding, 200
organization, document, 3
    cause-and-effect format, 19
    chunking, 144
    compare-and-contrast format, 18
    division-of-information format, 16–17
    of drafts, checklist, 86
    of e-mails, 176
    Idea Maps as a means of, 7, 12, 25, 55

in informational writing, 52
through power numbering, 49, 50, 65, 90
problem and solution format, 20
testing your, 50–52
Osder, Elizabeth,, 188
outline, formal, 4–6, 22, 75

P

Page, Susan (quote), 103
page design, 143
paragraphs.
    body, 66
    brief, 108, 124
    converting power sentences into, 42–43
    introductory, 55, 56
    one-sentence, 119
    Power 1, 60, 62, 65, 66, 67, 68, 69, 70, 86
    Power 2, 44, 66, 86
    Power 3, 45, 66, 86
    practice, 45–47
    reviewing, 50
parentheses, 135
Parker, Dorothy (quotes), 136, 140
Pascal, Blaise (quote), 153
passive voice, 94–96, 97–98, 183
pedantic writing / language, 23, 79–81, 170, 183
persuasive writing, 200, 203, 212
Peter, Lawrence (quote), 116
phrase, Zero Power, 61. *See also* words and phrases
Plain Language initiative and Web site, 77
Plimpton, George, 71
power numbering, 24, 27–29, 30–31, 36, 42–43, 49–50, 54, 55, 90
    Concluding Power 1, 23
    in e-mails, 179–181, 182
    free-writing and, 37
    in group, 74
    practice with, 32–35, 84, 86
    in professional reports, 166
    for proposal writing, 173–174
    in sales writing, 197
    short stories recommending, 48–49

to support details, examples, anecdotes, 49
tip for, 35
power paragraphs
in body of document, 66
converting sentences into, 42–43, 44–45
in document endings, 66–68, 69, 70
introductory, 65
practice, 45–47
power-selling, 198, 203–204, 208, 209, 212, 223–224, 237
power sentences
combining, 115
in document beginnings, 65
in document endings, 66–68, 69
practice, 40–42, 47, 70, 85
writing, 36, 65
practice, 89. See also C.L.E.V.R. solutions, 89
prefixes, 159
prepositions, ending sentence with, 120
press releases, 163–164
example, 164–165
price, in sales, 213–214
problem solving, idea mapping and, 22
productivity, idea mapping to achieve, 5
professional reports, 165–168
project management
e-mails for, 186
idea mapping for, 22
pronouns, 84–85, 138
proofreading, 127, 128
e-mails, 176, 183
formatting, 142
tip, 129
proposals, 173–174
conclusions in, 69
psychology, sales writing, 229–236
public service announcements, 69
punctuation, 115–116, 129, 187, 189
purpose of document, 9, 58, 66, 71, 184, 242 (Appendix)
"pushing buttons," 233–234, 236, 238

Q

quotation marks, 135–136
quotes, memorable, 74

R

ragged-right margins, 143, 152
reader. *See also* audience
    building rapport/connecting with, 63, 73, 86, 99, 118, 173,
        177
    focusing on, 9, 36, 223, 242 (Appendix)
    knowing your, 56, 57–58, 161
    motivating 200
    sales / marketing to, 222, 224
    tips regarding, 63
Reader Meter (Appendix), 242
reports, 173
    checklist when writing, 168
    conclusions in, 69
restating main points, 67
résumé tip, 114
revising, 72
rewriting, 39, 55, 71–72, 73–75, 87
    for clarity, 90–91, 93, 94–96
    for reader focus, 222–223
    pedantic phrases, 81
    redundant phrases, 109
    sales copy, 235
RFP (request for proposal), 175, 198
Roget's International Thesaurus, 74
rules
    to break, 118–120
    writing, 4–5, 116–118

S

SabreMark, Inc., 219
sales letter. *See* letters; sales writing
sales letters, 158–160
    checklist, 205–206
    example, 204–205, 206–208
sales pitch, 164

example, 61
in proposals , 173
sales psychology, 229–236
sales theory, new, 202–204, 237
sales writing, 199–201, 202, 236, 237, 237
   and cave story, 200–201
   checklist, 205–206
   cost-benefit analysis in, 206, 207–208, 209, 224
   features versus benefits in, 215, 217
   goals, 225–228
   Idea Map for, 216, 217, 223
   and power-selling, 203–204
   practice, 204–205, 210–212, 215–216, 219, 228, 236, 239–
      240
   reader-focused, 222–223
   rules, 225
   teamwork in, 203
   tips, 204, 206, 207, 209, 212, 214, 221, 224, 227, 230, 233
Schultz, Charles M. (quote), 231
semicolon, 153–154
sentence(s). *See also* Zero Power sentences
   building, 55
   combining, 114–115
   crisp, 98
   fragments, 118
   length, 107
   power, 36, 40–42, 66, 67, 69, 70, 86, 115
   rewriting, 93, 96, 112–113
   structure, parallel, 113–114
   structure, varying, 111–113
   writing concluding/ending, 70
   Zero Power, 61, 62, 163
sequencing, through power numbering, 49
sexist language, 101
similes, 103–104
Singer, Isaac (quote), 71
The Soul of a New Machine (Kidder), 52
spell-check, 140
spelling, 140–142, 187, 189
Stanley, Sir Henry Morton (quote), 131
Steinbeck, John (quote), 37
Stevenson, Robert Louis (quotes, 21, 90

structure. *See* organization
Strunk, William, Jr., 75
summarizing / summaries
    example, 67
    in professional reports, 167

T
target
    audience, 57, 58
    market, 218, 219–220, 221
teamwork, guided, 202–203, 237
technical writing, 109
templates, 147, 148, 152. *See also* letters
thank you messages/letters, 65, 162–163
Thatcher, Margaret (quote), 133
there, eliminating, 9
time management in writing, 186
time management habits (example), 8, 10, 11, 12 (Figures 1–4),
        27, 41, 44
    and power phrases and sentences, 36–37, 41
    with Power 1 paragraphs, 60
    with Power 1 sentences, 36–37, 41, 60
    with Power 2 paragraphs, 44, 115
    with Power 2 sentences, 36–37
    with Power 3 paragraphs, 45–47
    steps, 245–248 (Appendix)
    using Zero Power sentences
Todd, Jonathan, 195
to-do lists, 44, 46
tone, 57, 86
    in blogs, 189
    in e-mails, 184–185, 187
    in executive summaries, 170
    positive, 116–117, 157
    tip, 124
transitions in writing, 50–51, 66, 82, 243–244 (Appendix)
    e-mails, 183
    examples, 83
    tricky, 83–86
Travel & Leisure Magazine excerpt, 234–235
Twain, Mark (quotes), 79, 91, 130, 131, 132, 133, 134

typography, 143–144

U
underlining, in typography, 143

V
variety in writing, 111
verbs
    strong, 108
    to be, 92, 93–96
Verdi, Bob (quote), 103
voice (writing), 24, 76
    active versus passive, 94–96, 97–98, 183
    in blogs, 189

W
Wagner, Nancy J., 161–162
Web sites, developing, 161–162
Webster's Collegiate Dictionary, 74
Wells, H.G. (quote), 72
West, Mae (quote), 134
Wheatley, Margaret (quote), 6
White, E.B. (quotes), 72, 73, 152
Wikipedia, 188
Winstead, Lizz (quote), 134
win-win sales writing, 202, 237. *See also* sales writing
words
    action, 69
    endings, 107
    inventive, 119
    modifying, 108
    negative, 117
    precise, 99
    redundancy, 108, 109
    repetition, 84
    signatures, 84
    syllables in, 107
    transition, 82–83
    weasel, 92–93
words and phrases, using, 32, 34, 36, 108

writing/writer. *See also* sales writing
    business, 199
    checklist, 86, 191
    clarity in, 90–95
    on demand, 2
    descriptive, 102
    economy of, 106
    e-mail, 177, 186
    group, 74
    lazy, 92
    like you talk, 75–76, 77, 79, 80, 124
    organizing, 3
    outlining rules for, 4–5
    pedantic, 23, 79–81, 170, 183
    personality in, 76
    persuasive, 198, 200
    power selling in, 203–204
    power sentences, 40–42
    simplifying, 90
    technical, 76, 109
    time involved in, 3, 190
    tips, 80, 106
    tone, 76
    variety in, 111
    voice, 76
    Zero Power sentences (practice), 61

Y

Yeats, William, 66
you/your, using, 64, 117–118, 158

Z

Zero Power sentences, 24, 58–59, 62, 65
    combining, 115
    in e-mails, 181–182
    examples of, 60, 61
    practice writing, 61–63
    in press releases, 163
    tips, 61, 64
Zinsser, William (quote), 87

About Dr. Julie Miller &
Business Writing That Counts! ™

Dr. Julie Miller, founder and president of **Business Writing That Counts!**, is a best-selling international author, business consultant, trainer, and sought-after speaker. She has shared her proprietary three-step writing system with thousands of individuals in Fortune 500 companies.

Dr. Miller and her certified associates present a series of exciting hands-on strategic business writing workshops designed to help your organization save money instantly *and* increase productivity in quantifiable ways. These interactive, fast-paced, onsite and online sessions present timesaving techniques along with immediately adoptable strategies to produce quality documents and enhanced written communications. The result? Your management and staff will write with more speed and confidence, and *in less time*.

Business Writing That Counts! also offers one-on-one coaching, document review, a pre- and post-assessment of writing skills, and a subscription service for monthly writing tips. Clients range from city governments to banks to accounting firms, from insurance companies to manufacturers to software companies. Clients include: Microsoft, PACCAR, Key Bank, Analysis Group, Washington Mutual Bank, Cisco Systems, T-Mobile, the City of Seattle, U.S. Bank, Corbis, Moss Adams.

Please contact us for more information about products and professional services from **Business Writing That Counts!** ™
15401 NE 177th Drive
Suite 100
Woodinville, WA 98072
Call: 425-485-3221
Fax: 425-481-3197
E-mail: Julie@DrJulieMiller.com
Web site: www.businesswritingthatcounts.com

About **Jonathan Todd &** **SabreMark, Inc.**

Jonathan Todd — President & CEO, SabreMark, Inc.
Jonathan Todd is president & CEO of SabreMark, Inc. During the past two decades, Mr. Todd has personally handled or directed marketing for thousands of firms ranging from one person start-ups to the Fortune 500.

Mr. Todd has been recognized and retained by the government of the United States, foreign governments, Ministries of Trade and Economics, and FDIC Insured Banks. The Small Business Administration (SBA) commissioned him to produce special marketing and sales training materials for its agency. He has received over 50 separate Web design, marketing or e-commerce awards for excellence.

Mr. Todd has an extensive background in image licensing and marketing for the recording industry. Clients include #1 Billboard, Grammy-award-winning stars. He also has been the producer for over 50 recordings and holds both Producer and Executive Producer credits on numerous commercial CDs.

Mr. Todd specializes in building short-term marketing plans designed to boost profits without increasing advertising expenditures. His unusual ability to pinpoint issues and rapidly create viable marketing and sales solutions is in part due to his unique training experiences with thousands of firms representing every type of product and service. Mr. Todd resides in California with his wife and daughter.

Have a question? Wish you could speak with Jonathan about your individual needs? If you've enjoyed the special section **Business Writing That Sells!** and would like to discuss applying this information to your specific selling or marketing situation, feel free to send an e-mail to info@SabreMark.net with "Individual Assistance" in the Subject. Jonathan Todd or his staff will attempt to answer all inquiries as time permits. Be sure to include your name, telephone, city/country, e-mail, company name and any background information. We can't accept attachments so please confine your discussion to the body of your e-mail. For a faster response, visit our Web site *questions page* at http://www.sabremark.net/questions.htm.

SabreMark, Inc. has an extensive Web site with valuable information available at no charge. Visit http://www.SabreMark.net (and make sure you have any pop-up blockers disabled).

If you're interested in exploring a professional relationship with Jonathan Todd or the SabreMark team, please feel free to contact us via the following methods:

Call: (818) 865-9993

E-mail: Info@SabreMark.net (please write "Services" in the subject)

Write: Jonathan Todd

SabreMark, Inc.

5737 Kanan Road, #237

Agoura Hills, CA 91301

Special Resources
(See Below for Free Online Demo)

We have **five** companion business and sales writing online modules. These self-paced and interactive courses deepen your learning by reinforcing skills through exercises, activities and individualized feedback on your writing. A certified writing assessor reviews your work in each module, providing you with subjective support and specific suggestions on what works and what doesn't. The online descriptions follow:

Business Writing That Counts! **(Module I)**
Want to reduce your writing time and still produce powerful prose? This interactive self-study seminar presents Dr. Miller's unique three-step numbering system that can be used *no matter* what you have to write. Along with strategies to create clearer, simpler and more compelling documents, you will learn how to immediately get writing.

Take Your Writing to the Next Level! **(Module II)**
You will go beyond the level you are now and learn techniques that the professionals use. The end result will be writing that targets your reader so that your message comes through loud and clear. Convey professionalism by mastering new strategies and make your letters, manuals, newsletters, proposals, e-mails grab attention with sharp and proactive sentences. From simple rules that guarantee simplicity to proofing your work for error-free documents, you will gain career-enhancing skills.

Idea Mapping: Your Shortest Route to Fast, Effective Writing! **(Module III)**
Have you ever calculated the amount of time you waste getting organized with a writing project? Overcome this hurdle and recapture the time by using *Idea Mapping for Writing*—the shortest distance between an idea and a finished product. Learn how to quickly organize your thoughts by

creating a fast physical blueprint before writing. Based on the latest brain research, these powerful and proven techniques can cut your organizing time down to minutes. This process can be applied throughout your writing project. This module teaches you how to instantly give structure to your ideas while helping you unlock your creative genius.

Punctuation That Counts! (Module IV)

Who you are and what you stand for—your very credibility—is reflected in your documents. Not taking the time to make it right is akin to not dressing appropriately for an important client. Your client? Your reader! Take the same care with your written communications. Review proper punctuation and capitalization to ensure accurate comprehension for your readers. Boost your confidence and your readers' confidence in *you.*

Sales Writing That Counts! (Module V)

This is an extension of the concepts taught by Jonathan Todd in the Sales section of this book. Understand the difference between communicating and selling. You will learn the psychology of how opinion is molded by words into motivation for the reader. Then you will be provided with templates for writing that gets sales results. You will learn how to communicate—whether it's proposals, e-mails or brochures—to influence or alter a reader's position on any topic, any time, anywhere.

Note: For some of these modules, undergraduate/graduate and CPE credits are available.

Go to www.businesswritingthatcounts.com and/or e-mail us Julie@drjuliemiller.com to request a **free online demo.**

Corporate discounts for volume licenses to the online modules are available. Contact the Corporate Services division at (425) 485-3221 for inquiries.

Order Form

QTY.	Title	Price U.S	Canada	Total
	Business Writing That Counts!	$24.95	$32.95	
	Add $6.00 for Shipping and Handling			
	Add $1.00 for each additional book			
	Sales tax (WA state residents add sales tax)			
	Total enclosed			

Telephone Orders:
(425) 485-3221

Fax Order:
425-481-3197
Fill out this form and fax.

Postal Orders:
Business Writing That Counts!
15401 NE 177th Drive
Suite 100
Woodinville, WA 98072

**For Sales & Marketing
Consultation/Executive Services**
Jonathan Todd/SabreMark, Inc
E-mail: info@SabreMark.net
Phone: (818) 865-9993

E-mail Orders
E-mail your order request to
Julie@DrJulieMiller.com

Web Site Orders
www.businesswritingthatcounts.com
click on book cover

**For Product or Services inquiries
Business Writing That Counts!**
Onsite or online training:
E-mail: Julie@DrJulieMiller.com

Payment Method (check one)
❑   Check
❑   Visa
❑   MasterCard
❑   American Express

Name on card_____

Card #_____

Expiration Date_____Billing Zip Code_____

Signature_____
Ship to:
   Name_____

   Address_____

   City_____State_____Zip_____

   Phone (   ) _____Fax_____

Quantity discounts available. Call (425) 485-3221